ARE YOU ESSENTIAL?

SIMPLE SECRETS TO UNLOCKING YOUR TRUE POTENTIAL, RELEASING THE PAST AND TAPPING INTO YOUR PASSION & PURPOSE

CINDY HOPE

CONTENTS

THE DAILY AFFIRMATIONS CHECKLIST

(Never start your day without it…)

What you speak over yourself and your life affects your brain, body and circumstances. Starting today you need to Speak LIFE! I have made this very easy for you with this daily checklist of positive affirmations.

This checklist includes:

❏ 20 Powerful Affirmations to say to change your life

To receive your Affirmations checklist, visit the link:

www.cindyhopesays.com

INTRODUCTION

*"To be **yourself** in a world that is constantly trying to make you something else is the greatest accomplishment."*

— UNKNOWN

Every news station was playing the same thing on repeat, "A pandemic had hit the world! The coronavirus!" There were many "unknown" answers to all the questions circling about the supposedly deadly virus that virtually everyone was in panic mode. Anxiety was climbing, people didn't know what was in store for them, and, without a doubt, nobody knew how long this would last. Heck, even science didn't have the answers.

Then came the announcement everyone had been dreading. It was like out of a sci-fi movie or one of those apocalyptic doomsday films we've grown accustomed to. "Everyone is to STAY HOME, quarantined unless you are ESSENTIAL!" These words became the national anthem. You heard it on the radio, TV commercials, talk shows, and all over social media. Musicians from all over the world composed songs about the pandemic, urging everyone to stay at home and maintain social distancing, unless of course, they are essential.

Obviously, we understood the big picture and why they did what they did— but what we couldn't see initially was the devastating impact this would have on many. "Are you ESSENTIAL?" These words stung my heart because I know that beyond what people do for a living—there is a cry in each person's soul—to know if they are "essential."

Dealing with doubts, insecurities, and feelings of worth-lessness can cripple your life if you aren't taught how to over-come and be the essential person this world needs you to be. Sadly, we aren't taught how to be the best versions of ourselves, look out for our interests, and be fulfilled. Instead, we learn how to please others and do whatever will make them happy from a young age. Think of that child who wants to impress her parents.

"Are you essential?" reminded me of a time when I asked the same question of myself. It was a pivotal moment, a defining time in which I faced my doubts, my past, and the identity I wore for others. I had to choose to grow through it and find my passion and truth.

Change is essential for everyone's growth and develop-ment. Without it, you will stay where you are, doing the same thing you've always done, expecting more but achieving nothing. For some people, that's a good thing. They are fulfilling their dreams and are happy with how things are.

But, when you are terrible to yourself and relentlessly compare yourself to others, it's not the same. You wake up looking for evidence that you are a nobody that nobody cares about you, and that you aren't good enough. If you were, you would feel different and be different. Your life wouldn't be in shambles and it wouldn't be so hard to be comfortable in your own skin.

So, you walk around feeling there is something wrong with you because you are still single and every guy you meet is the proverbial frog. That's why your boss hates you or why you can't hold down a job for more than a month. Even your parents agree and your social circle is made up of two people who, like you, hate themselves. You live in the wrong neighborhood, drive an old worn-out car, and hate that you earn so little.

What you don't realize is you can't hate yourself into a version you love. You can't tear your self-esteem apart and expect to feel confident, walking with your head high. And, what most people don't know is that everyone is watching how you treat yourself, so they can give you more of it. Don't expect to reap what you didn't sow. You get who you are, not what you want.

"Things don't change, we change."

If you want to change your life and your circumstances, you have to start by changing yourself. Not by buying more clothes and faking it until you make it, but by working on yourself and being that person you've always wanted to be today. Don't wait for tomorrow to be happy. Be happy today. Don't wait for tomorrow to start eating healthily. Start today.

But is it that simple? Obviously not, but there are tools you can use to help you stay on course. Ask yourself, are you good enough for what? For whom? What would you need to achieve to be good enough? To be essential? If you investigate this closely, you'll see that you are using guidelines that only exist because you have given them space and accommodation in your life and thoughts.

This part of you will never be satisfied and if you

continue down this road, you will keep trying to live your life pleasing it, until you decide to stop. You have to stand up for yourself and say that enough is enough. You have to choose to end the cycle because you can't do the same thing over and over again and expect different results. That's just not how it works.

Stop waiting for things to change; wake up and change. You can break free from these feelings and thoughts. Choose to stop allowing circumstances to dictate your worth. I've traveled this road before, and I know that although it's not the easiest of things, it's possible.

After years of pain, disappointment, and self-doubts, I made it out, and I'm going to walk with you until you do too. A blind man can't lead a blind man, but when one of you knows the way to success, it's easy to lead another. It doesn't matter where you are right now, how deep you've sunk into giving up. All that's required is a willingness to change and willpower that's strong enough to push you to go through the process.

So, buckle up and join the ride. And remember, the work won't be done for you. That is entirely up to you. If you want mountains to move, you just have to have faith as small as a mustard seed, and you'll see things start to change. Don't wait for others to work for you, because everything you need to change is inside of you. Look within and you will find the answers. I'm only here to guide you and my joy would be to see you on the other side, happy and comfortable in your own skin because you are enough. You are essential!

CHAPTER ONE: THE EPIDEMIC OF FEELING INADEQUATE

AS I LAY ON THE BATHROOM MAT CURLED UP, TRYING TO avoid any part of me touching the ice-cold floor, my tears seemed endless streaming down my face. For one moment, I was relieved to be on the mat so that it would soak up this mess, and I wouldn't have to clean up yet another thing!

How had I gotten here? How is it possible to be in so much pain without a visible wound? Not even a single one! My heart was broken; it felt like it hurt to breathe.

A little less than a year ago, I was happily married, or so I thought. I had a successful career, was a millionaire on paper by my own doing, and well on my way to achieving all the goals that I thought defined a successful life. I had designed this bathroom, everything from the tile, towels, and matching rugs. It was supposed to be our dream home. A happy place where we share love, joy, and overcome challenges that come with the package called life. Not to sound cliché, but it was meant to be "my little heaven on earth."

As I managed to sit myself up on the floor, I gazed outside the window only to see the "Foreclosure" sign hanging in the yard. The tears started again. I was divorced, broke, and a failure... at least these were the words I whispered through a deep sigh.

Every insecurity, self-doubt, and fear surfaced through the pain like old friends whom I hadn't seen in years, but seemed to pick up right where they left off, terrorizing my mind. I guess I thought success and marriage would kill those thoughts, but all they had done was to bury them until now.

Perhaps everyone would finally see through this mask I was wearing. To everyone, I was confident, loved, and an iron woman who held the world in her hands. Instead, I was the consummate failure at love, full of doubts, and wondered what my real purpose in life was!

I felt empty.

Rock bottom or "bathroom floor bottom" is where my journey really started. As I began to read, study, and learn about everything from the brain, the mind, emotions, and how people affect us and the control we have, I began to heal and grow.

If you are ready for change and desire to live your life genuinely whole and fulfilled, stick with me through these pages and **do** what is asked, don't just read. There is healing and growth for all.

We begin our journey together by facing the epidemic of feeling inadequate.

A few decades ago, people did not have the kind of tech we have today. In fact, our forefathers had to rely on smoke signals to send a message before the postman became an icon. Today, you quickly text someone an email, send them a text message, or make a quick call if you need to speak to someone miles away. The level of technological advancement we experience today is so high that life has been made easier and more efficient.

While life has been made easier to some degree, human beings have become busier. Instead of slowing down and doing less, now that most of the things are handled for us, we have convinced ourselves that we need to fill this time with more activities. In fact, we are busier today than our forefathers were, even busier than people were a few decades ago.

Think about it. Today, you have to work harder to maintain the level of life you are used to, probably working two or more jobs a day and sleeping less than the required eight hours a day to make ends meet. While there is great advancement, you have more bills to pay to enjoy some of the developments invented on earth. You probably have a few subscriptions you need to maintain on top of regular bills, and you need a savings account to cater for a rainy day. Obviously, you also want to go for an exquisite holiday in the Maldives or Cancun, and buy a diamond ring for the love of your life.

If you have kids, you want to take them to the best schools, so they are set for life; you want to ensure they don't suffer as much as you did growing up. So, you do everything in your power to ensure they have enough toys, enjoy the little luxuries you didn't receive as a kid, and give them more freedom to enjoy screen time and work less.

But, deep down, you know you can never do enough, and sometimes, seated by yourself, you know you can't be and do everything you'd want to. For instance, that holiday will set you back a couple of thousands of dollars and may leave you in debt if you take it this year. While you have managed to save something, you are sure you can't compete with Susan from marketing who is flying her family to Paris this year while you'll be spending the holidays in your parent's wooden cabin... again! There is always something reminding you that you can't do or be enough, no matter how hard you try.

People may credit you for the ability to move forward and let go quickly, but you still feel sorry for yourself, and you may even be convinced that you'll never be good enough. Some days, you allow these thoughts to dominate and make you feel like a horrible human being who deserves to be burned at the stake, but, sometimes, you feel like a superhero complete with the "s" on your chest.

Think of that 21-year-old going in for their first interview. While they know they need the job and that it will help them build their work experience and have something meaningful to show on their resume, they probably can't stop fidgeting even before entering the interview room. Smartly dressed in their only suit, they stroll towards the smiling interviewers who, with every effort possible, try to make them feel at ease. But the nerves won't let the candidate relax.

At the back of his mind, they feel like they aren't good enough or don't deserve it. Surely there must be someone else who will do a better job than them. Why would they even consider them when they are just fresh from college? All they have to show is a crappy internship that's meaningless anyway. When they receive the rejection letter, three little words seem to be more pronounced in a single sentence. "*If they don't believe* they are good enough, why should we?"

These scenarios are not new to you and I. I'm sure there are times you feel that you don't deserve the good things happening in your life, or maybe you always tell yourself, "I'm not good enough, I don't deserve this." Think of the promotions you have bypassed because you thought, "I won't get it anyway," or the fact that you've been in an unfulfilled relationship for so long because you think "I can't get someone better." Even when people cross your boundaries, you let them because "Why stand up for yourself ? It won't work anyway."

Psychology notes that this is not a feeling but a thought

that comes from our inner critic and is often something we develop when we are young. As adults, it's easy to comprehend these four little words (I'm not good enough), but freeing ourselves emotionally from them is a journey that takes work. Before we get to how to overcome these feelings, let's first consider how we internalize them so much that they become so deeply ingrained in us, like part of our identity.

Let's go back to when you were a little kid. As a child, you had one job; to soak up and internalize what you learned as you try to understand the world around you. The most important thing to you, as with any child, was to gain the love, approval, and affection of your primary caregiver. You didn't understand why people behave in a certain way or do what they do. All you cared about was to be loved.

If you grew up in a family where your parents were not always available, either because they traveled too much for work, were alcoholics, or narcissists, you may have failed to understand their actions. For instance, you didn't know why your parents would one day rely on alcohol, why they are only available a few days a week, or why they didn't show empathy and love. You didn't understand why your parents never had time for you even when they were back from a business trip. Or why they'd prefer to spend most of their time working late, answering emails, and attending online meetings instead of sharing a warm meal with you.

In abusive families, kids fail to understand why the adults are acting so horribly or why they don't stop to consider how that affects them. Now, remember, your need is to be loved, accepted, and shown affection. In these instances, you begin to try and fix the adult's problem and, in turn, receive the love and care you crave and deserve. That's why kids will often say things like, "If I did better at school, my parents wouldn't fight," or "If I earned money, my parents wouldn't have to work so hard." Maybe you've heard some kids say, "If

I was better at sports, my dad/mom wouldn't drink so much because they would be at my games," or something along those lines.

You see, kids are smart; like sponges, they absorb the environment on an emotional, physical, and mental level. At a very young age, kids learn that if their parents are happy, the home will be filled with love, laughter, and joy and they will, in turn, be happy. That's why little girls or boys will say, "When daddy isn't mad and fighting with mom, he is nice to all of us. He brings us gifts and does everything for us."

So, if your childhood home was not happy, you may have tried to fix the situation by being a better kid, and when that didn't work, you tried the opposite by being a bad child, so your parents may focus on you.

Now, let's think of a little child who wants to fix adult problems. Obviously, you will fail miserably, and the more you fail and try again, the more you internalize that it doesn't matter what you do, you can't fix your parents' problems. Of course, you are a kid and can't fix problems, but that's not what your brain tells you. Remember, you can't fully understand the world around you and only see it through the lenses provided by your parents. You don't know you can't fix the problem, or that it's not your fault or business to try and fix things. So, you keep trying and failing and reinforcing the thoughts and feelings that you won't succeed no matter what you do.

Without knowing, though not all the time, parents also blame or project on their kids the negative feelings they are feeling. Narcissists, for instance, do this all the time. If a parent self-loathes, they may project this on their child instead of healing and accepting themselves for who they are. As a child, through your true nature of absorbing everything in your environment, you learn this behavior. You start thinking that it's your fault your parents don't love you. You must be unlovable because if you were loveable, your parents would spend more time with you, love you, and show affection. You end up carrying a lot of emotional baggage from your family, taking on a burden you can't handle.

If this was your childhood, you might begin to see some instances that may have led to your thinking that you aren't good enough. If your father was a businessman, for example, and, for whatever reason, his business never seemed to grow, you may have tried to fix it by offering advice on what he can do, so his business thrives. If the business continued to worsen, you might have blamed yourself because your idea didn't work. Your father probably never tried your approach, but because you nagged him about it so much, he said he tried it and it didn't work.

Now that you are a grown-up and understand that each family has its own set of dysfunctions, it doesn't mean all the effects have been erased from your life. The negative messages of "I couldn't fix the problem. I wasn't good enough, and I'm not good enough today," remain with you.

OTHER REASONS INCLUDE:

1. You had critical, demanding, or aloof parents.

You may have had a good childhood, lived in a nice neighborhood, went to a good school, joined the drama club, and even won a science contest. But you still craved the approval and love that every child needs from its parents. Maybe your parents wanted you to be faster when running track, work harder on your spelling, or be a better dancer. They may have favored your sibling, or whatever message that made you feel like you weren't good enough.

2. Your caregivers could not offer stability, safety, or security.

In some cases, the caregiver cannot give the child the security, support, and stability they need to thrive. Maybe your parents were alcoholic, suffered from acute depression, or were in a toxic relationship that took up all their time and attention, so they had none left for you. You may, for instance, feel responsible for your parents' happiness.

3. You experienced intense trauma in the past

Not all reasons for developing a negative self-image are associated with your parents. Childhood trauma is another culprit. It's defined as an event, environment, or situation experienced during childhood that left you feeling vulnerable, and like you couldn't count on the world around you to be safe. Trauma has a way of affecting how you think about yourself and how you relate to others. Most kids feel that the traumatic event was their fault and that they could have done better.

Childhood trauma doesn't involve physical events only, but includes anything that made you feel alone, overwhelmed, terrified, and vulnerable as a kid. It could be anything from the loss of a loved one, a natural disaster, an accident, moving to another country, living in poverty, a surgery, humiliation at school, being neglected, being putdown and shamed by parents and others, and suffering physical abuse.

SIGNS THAT YOU BELIEVE YOU AREN'T GOOD ENOUGH

You may already suspect that you feel like you aren't good enough, whether you acknowledge it to others or yourself.

There are a few common tell-tale signs about how you feel. Now, just because these signs ring true to you doesn't mean you aren't good enough, far from it. They simply mean that that's how you feel. If I could emphasize that by sprinkling it in glitter and flashing lights, I would, so keep it in mind as you read this section.

1. Feeling empty

Do you ever get that empty feeling in your stomach? How do you interpret it? Often, it's taken as a sign that things aren't ok, and most people proceed to cover it up with a large margarita, pizza, a bottle of wine and/or a tub of ice cream and anything else that will briefly alleviate this feeling. But what does this really feel like? If you don't spend time reading theories and the latest research on the topic, it may sound a little metaphysical and confusing.

Empty can feel like a terrible underlying pressure or some kind of tension. It may manifest in a fundamental fear of being and feeling alone that sits with you momentarily or through everyday life. By definition, being alone means feeling frightened; that's often explained as something close to losing yourself or falling apart. It's hard to describe feeling empty, but I'm sure you get the picture or have experienced these feelings yourself.

When they don't turn to food, most people tend to turn to someone else who might answer why they are feeling the way they are. Sometimes, this person can't or won't offer the expected support, either because of their unreasonable expectations or because people are demanding the wrong answer. They just can't help it.

This dependence on others is dangerous and taxing. Although you need others to help you by providing feedback and reflecting on your feelings and ideas, it often feels like your life depends on it. You may even live in this cycle where you are happy, then sad, then you talk to someone, eat, or drink and then feel better about yourself for a while before it all comes crashing down on you again.

Emptiness manifests differently in different people and varies in intensity. It can be hard to identify, especially when combined with grief. Unlike sadness, despair, or hopelessness, emptiness often feels like the absence of feelings. That's why you search for answers or feel that your work or life lacks meaning or importance. Why, what, and when you experience this depends on your personality, life circumstances, and events. For instance, you may feel empty and alone if you value relationships, and your esteem may suffer if you value power, but your ego isn't boosted by aggression, power, and success.

2. Continually asking yourself what others will think

"What will they think?" Does this question crop up in your life more often than you'd like to admit? It doesn't matter if you are working on a project at work, meeting a blind date, your girlfriend's parents, or starting a business. You focus more on what others think than what lights up and feels right and true to you at the moment, not knowing that this is feeding into your limiting beliefs.

You can't predict or control the future, which may make you worry about what others will think about the things you do, your choices, and even how you look. Let's be clear, though. There is nothing wrong with wanting to make a good impression and project a positive persona to the world. If your decisions and preferences are made after careful consideration of what others will think, then you are losing authenticity and what's true to you. If you notice the following habits, you may be a victim of this.

- You try to please everybody

Think about it. How much time and effort do you spend pleasing everybody? Do you want to win everybody over so you don't have a conflict with anyone? Maybe you even do some things not because you want to, but because you don't want to make your friend, boss, parents, or spouse angry. What about when making decisions? Do you spend time seeking other people's opinions such that it takes you more time to decide what to do than it should have? Or do you spend time figuring out which decisions will be agreeable to everyone? Besides taking too much energy, you end up making a decision that doesn't consider your true desires.

- Other people's needs come before yours

Ever met a new mom when going out shopping? You can be sure that her cart will have 90% of baby items and other things the family needs, and only 10% of what she needs. Heck, she may even disregard what she needs to buy a few items for someone else. This mom rarely spends time doing what she loves, but she is always busy taking care of others. She ensures the family is cared for, meets her clients' and boss' demands at work, and goes the extra mile to meet her friend's expectations of her, even when she knows it hurts her. Your case may not be as extreme as this moms' is, but you may be in the same predicament, losing yourself in the shadow of meeting other people's needs while neglecting your own. Emotionally, you are telling yourself that everybody matters more than you do.

- You feel guilty when you do something for yourself

Now, let's assume someone calls you and wants help with something, but for the first time in a long time, you say "no" because you want to go skiing. Immediately after refusing, you feel so guilty that you don't even enjoy your hobby. Things may be so uncomfortable that you end up tossing your hobby aside to help your friend. You end up caring too much about what your friend will think, but slowly, you are losing your truth.

- You tell a lot of white lies

Because you don't want to disappoint others, you prefer to tell a few white lies here and there to keep everyone happy. For instance, because you really want to ski, you tell your friend that your boss just called you to the office so you can't help them with their thing. When you feel your opinions and ideas are not respected, you tell a white lie, so you fit into whatever conversation or group you are with.

- You are a social chameleon

You probably know someone who changes their personality when they interact with different people. For instance, they even change their political party when they are hanging out with a particular crowd. Or maybe they morph into something just to fit into a social environment. This means they care too much about what others say and think about them.

3. You seek certainty

Naturally, we all live for certainty. We want to be sure that everything will be alright and work out in our favor. This need naturally makes us want to control every situation.

Think about it. You know what you want, how you want it, and when you prefer to get it. Anything outside of that feels unnatural, scary, and foreign. Because you know what's best, you want to micro-manage every aspect of your life, just to ensure nothing goes wrong.

The flip side is, you plan for the worst-case scenario, so you have a plan B, C, and maybe even D. This comes with a lot of pressure, which leads to frustration. Also, is micro-managing everything as effective as you'd like it to be? Probably not, and this is exactly the problem. You not only miss out on being present, but the constant failure only reinforces the feelings and thoughts that you aren't good enough.

Now that we know where the feeling of "not good enough" comes from and the signs to watch out for, let's consider what you need to do to overcome these thoughts. But first, we need to highlight a few fallacies you must be made aware of.

FALLACIES OF "NOT GOOD ENOUGH"

1. "Enough" can be defined

I'm sure you must have wondered what would qualify as "good enough." You may even have an idea and think, "I may be good enough if I didn't snap at my kids... If I had money... If I lost some weight." But, can you define what will make you enough? Let's use money as our example to illustrate the point.

If you grew up in poverty or wanting to amass a lot of wealth, you will work hard at your job or start a company. Eventually, if you are consistent and follow good business practices, you will make the money you desire.

Now, let's assume you are a millionaire and money is not

a problem. You have enough, such that you spend freely without worrying where your next paycheck will come from. You are also committed to your spiritual journey, and you don't procrastinate. Generally, these three (money, procrastination, and spiritual journeys) are the primary "items" we use to measure being enough.

So, you have all the money you would ever need, have a great spiritual relationship, don't snap or yell at your kids, and never procrastinate. Now what? Are you enough, or are you still lacking to some degree?

Let's scrutinize your inner thoughts and feelings. Deep down, even with all these in check, you still feel as empty as you did when you were poor. You always seek other people's approval, try to please those around you, and feel lonely when you are at a party surrounded by friends. You may even be dancing as you try to hold back tears from your eyes.

The idea of being enough is undefinable, and the boundaries are loose and impermeable. You can't use the same measure to define "enough" for every Tom, Dick, and Harry, the same way feelings of not being enough vary from person to person.

> 2. Understanding where you first started feeling that you aren't good enough will automatically enable you to believe that you are good enough.

This isn't entirely false. In fact, we will delve into this subject in the next chapter because it's a vital piece of the "I'm not good enough" puzzle. But, knowing the genesis of your thought will only be helpful if you take action and when you first seek to understand the message-bearer's pain when they inflicted this thought onto you. Most people who teach others that they aren't good enough only do so because they believe that they themselves aren't good enough. Also, some don't do it intentionally.

We won't be advocating for you to scream at them and tell them off so you can overcome your thoughts, or tell you that the message-bearer can't be trusted because they were a screw-up (in the case of alcoholic or narcissistic parents). From my experience, that doesn't work. Remember, most message-bearers are people we love unconditionally and respect and people who meant well for us. Their messages may be garbage, but if you look closely enough, they meant to help, not to hurt. If you use any of these methods, you are responding to abuse by becoming an abuser. You don't need more harm in your life.

3. Finding evidence of your enough-ness and using affirmations will help you feel good enough

The major problem with this method is that it buys back into trying to define good enough. That's why you may try to find evidence that you are good enough. Eventually, your brain becomes addicted to using evidence, and you have to keep finding it to feel good enough. When you don't find it, you go back to your default setting of believing that you aren't good enough. That's not what we are after here. We want to end the cycle and give you a new beginning.

Also, you don't need to find evidence because you already are—no proof required for that. Let's use an example to illustrate this better. You are standing in a room with a buffet, but you stand with your back to the table. Obviously, you can't see the food. Instead of turning around and serving your fill, you repeat "I have food" several times to yourself, hoping that the food will appear.

Instead, all you need to do is stop assuming that the food isn't there so you can see the buffet table right behind you. If you already feel that you aren't good enough, and repeat the affirmations "I'm good enough" several times a day, you are creating more of the thought and feeling of lack.

Deep down, every time you say your affirmations, your inner critic will be there to remind you, "that's not true. That's not what your emotions say. You know you aren't good enough." And instead of creating what you need, you enforce what you don't need.

Not to say that affirmations are useless and won't help you. Not at all. There is a place for affirmations, and I strongly believe in them, but only when they are used correctly.

I did promise you that we will look at some simple exercises you can start doing before delving deep into solving the "I'm not good enough puzzle," but before we do that, you need to realize and accept that you are not alone in this.

YOU ARE NOT ALONE

Imagine you are working, checking off boxes from your to-do list. When you get a new assignment, you dive right in and make sure you do it to the best of your ability, and every time you do, you emerge victorious. You always have a project at hand, achieving everything that's expected from you or more, but you still feel empty, numb, and like nobody understands you. You wonder when you will stop living to prove yourself, when you will feel complete, and experience the warmth of happiness and comfort.

In truth, everyone has gone through this at some point in their life. In fact, a whopping 85% of Americans have low self-worth and feel precisely the same way you do. They are consumed by fear of failure, tend to procrastinate, are angry, feel unfulfilled, unlovable, nervous, shy, can be quite indecisive, and suffer from other uncomfortable feelings and thoughts that deter them from realizing their full potential.

Yet, all they want is to be truly happy and comfortable in their own skin, feel valued and fulfilled, feel worthy of the many great things life has to offer, and easily cope with life's challenges. They want to be productive and have personal power while being accepted by others and be considered worthy. So, this is not a unique situation and although your feelings may vary from another person's, the ultimate goal is to feel great about yourself and be accepted.

DAILY EXERCISES TO FEEL GOOD ENOUGH

We will get into more details on overcoming these feelings, but I felt it's wise to give you a solid foundation and something you can work on right away. Because we will be going into in-depth details later, I will only highlight a few points so you can start working. Let's get to it.

1. Let go of the approval of others

If you are fond of seeking approval from other people, this should be your first step. You probably waste a lot of time caring about everyone else in the world except yourself. Live your life with integrity and be true to yourself and what makes you happy and excited to get out of bed in the morning. Worry only about what you think about something and ditch other people's opinions. You've heard the saying "Opinions are like belly buttons, everyone has one!" Well it's true, but you are not obligated to accept others' opinions. Your priority is to make yourself happy.

2. Show up and be your best

Your best will look different from another person's best, and that's ok. Make your peace with this fact and be comfortable. There will always be people ahead of you in life, the same way you are ahead of others, so stop comparing yourself and be the best version of yourself. Comparison is like cancer to contentment. Nothing will destroy your ability to be "happy" quicker than constantly comparing yourself to others. If you give 100 percent to your work, family, yourself, and those around you, you have done well and should feel good about it.

3. Surround yourself with likeminded people

This is an incredibly important point! When your inner critic is on high volume, surrounding yourself with people with the same problem will only magnify what you are going through. Instead, surround yourself with like-minded people, or people who already feel enough. These people will remind you that you are amazing, they will value your opinion, and even ask for your insight. They will pull you out of the rabbit hole when you fail and remind you of your true identity. This will make your work easier since you have a support system you can rely on. Eventually, you will learn to stand on your two feet. This principle should be applied to every aspect of your life. If you want to move ahead in business, find more successful people that can fit into your life and give you great advice. Being around them will inspire you to work harder and to follow in their footsteps. The same is true if you hang around people who are lazy and in and out of work because they keep taking days off to go to the beach. Soon your work ethic will deteriorate, and you will lose sight of your goals. So, check your circle!

4. Practice makes perfect

It doesn't happen in a day, the same way believing these thoughts didn't happen in a day. It will take time, patience, and self-acceptance. There isn't a perfect growth route, so don't look for one. Instead, be ready to rise and try again each time you fall. You can do it. You've got this!

CHAPTER SUMMARY

In this chapter, we have learned:

- That your past plays a major role in inflicting the pain that you are not enough.
- Feeling empty, asking what others will think, and seeking certainty are signs that you think you aren't good enough.
- "Enough" can't be defined, and understanding your past and saying affirmations are only part of what you need to heal.
- 85% of American suffer from low self-worth. You are not alone in this.
- Daily exercises you can do to work on your thoughts such as showing up and being your best every time.

In the next chapter you will learn how you can remove yourself from your self-imposed quarantine with the past, step out of your comfort zone, and finally start your healing process.

CHAPTER TWO: QUARANTINE WITH YOUR PAST

IT'S SUNDAY AFTERNOON, AND ALTHOUGH YOU DON'T always think about it, you want to plan the week. In general, your week will likely be more or less the same as last week, so there isn't much planning needed. You will see the same set of friends, go to the same job to do the same monotonous tasks you've grown accustomed to, and live in the same house. Pretty usual stuff.

You think about your distant future, but it seems a little murkier. You can't pinpoint where you will be, where you'll be living, working, or whether you'll have the same friends you currently do.

According to Kathleen Arnold, Karl Szpunar, and Kathleen McDermott in their paper "Memory and Cognition," your ability to envision your past remarkably influences the future. Your memories of past experiences are the basis of what you envision in the future.

Let's go back to when you were a child, right before you started thinking that you weren't good enough. When you were born, your brain wasn't fully developed, but you had the superpowers to collect information from your environment. You used this information to form beliefs that guide you to date. For instance, you may have seen your parents drink a lot and fight, and you thus learned to associate alcohol with violence.

Kids absorb information from their environment at such a high rate that, by the time they are six, they have formed and solidified thousands of beliefs in their minds that help them interact with the world around them. You were no different. These beliefs are the strongest factors influencing your personality. If your parents were fond of throwing fists when they were drunk, it doesn't mean you won't take a strong drink. But, your reaction after drinking will have different outcomes. You will be as violent as your parents were (or worse), or you will have your drinking under such control, so that you don't end up like them. Either way, the information you assimilate as a child helps you form the basis of this decision years later.

The feelings of "I'm not good enough" aren't different. According to Dr. Jonice Webb, Ph.D., in her book *Running on Empty: Overcome Your Childhood Emotional Neglect*, emotional neglect from your primary caregiver is the cause of your emptiness, vulnerability, and worry. Your past wreaks havoc in your daily life, even when you had a good childhood.

According to Webb, childhood emotional neglect in kids isn't the same as emotional abuse. It's a bit more subtle and harder to pinpoint, which makes it difficult to understand. When you were a child, your parents may have failed to see, know, or understand who you really were, but instead looked at you through what they thought and wanted you to be. Perhaps your parents were too busy and did not see you as the child you were. In some cases, childhood emotional abuse means a lack of rules, boundaries, and structure. It also manifests as lack of parental encouragement and inability to provide the tools you needed to navigate the world.

That's why you feel that you aren't good enough even when your parents provided for you physically, were loving, caring, and well-meaning.

That's why you:

- Judge yourself too harshly
- Don't really know who you are, what you like, or what you want
- Feel as if you have nothing left to give
- When you do say "no" you feel guilty about it
- You don't understand why you feel this way when you had a good childhood
- Feel like you are on the outside looking in
- Are lonely even in the company of others
- Are fiercely independent and won't ask for help even when you know you need it
- Can't manage your emotions
- Feel blue, but you can't tell why you feel this way

There are various reasons why your parents could have been emotionally neglectful. They probably didn't have a better model, didn't have enough emotional resources because they were overworked or overwhelmed, or struggled with their own emotions and mental health issues, such as grief and depression.

For instance, an authoritarian parent could have focused on rules, was overly strict, had no flexibility, and was demanding. They didn't listen to your feelings or consider your needs and didn't bother to explain why they set specific rules. Most abusive parents fall into this category. Make no mistake, though. Not all authoritarian parents are abusive, but you can bet most are emotionally neglectful.

Permissive parents are cool, enforce a few rules and boundaries, and are mostly fun and games. They fail to see that their kids need proper structures, rules, and limits. It's these boundaries and rules that kids use to define themselves. So, you may have been the envy of other kids in high school, but the lack of limits and structure is the very reason why you feel as if you aren't good enough.

We briefly mentioned narcissistic parents. These parents feel the world should revolve around them. They often present themselves as confident but are emotionally weak and get hurt easily. They usually make everything about their needs instead of what you need. Your parents may have thought, "What will everyone else think if they know you did A, B, or C?" Narcissists are often vindictive and judge others harshly.

Absent parents aren't always absent because they wish to be. Your parents may have died, had to work long hours to provide for the family, were ill, or got divorced. Maybe they had to spend most of the time caring for another child with special needs. You ended up raising yourself to a large extent and even raised your siblings if you have them. You didn't get a chance to talk about emotions or painful things happening at home, because you didn't want to stress your parents more. Although you are a responsible adult, you have few reserves for yourself.

Parents who were depressed or battling a mental health issue simply didn't have the bandwidth to parent, so you grew up feeling like you had to behave perfectly so you wouldn't make your parents feel worse. Addicts aren't necessarily dysfunctional and overtaken by their habits. It could be that they didn't have time for you because when you got home from school, they were on their third glass of wine, binge-watching movies, or busy gambling online to pay any attention to you. When they were sober, they were present and there for you, but they often neglected you to feed their addiction. Maybe they didn't abuse any drugs but were addicted to their work. These people are what psychologists call functional addicts.

I hope you are nodding by this point because you have an in-depth understanding of where this mess came from. Maybe you identify with one or a few of the scenarios mentioned above. Remember, the feelings of "I'm not good enough" aren't pegged on parental failure alone. Remember that bully in kindergarten who just couldn't leave you alone? Or that teacher who never seemed to be impressed no matter what you did? Maybe your childhood best friend dumped you for the popular girl's/boy's club. These, too, are instances that could have led to the muddy water you find yourself in today.

Now we will dive a little deeper into the subject and understand how our brains are wired and how they internalize these thoughts and feelings. This section will help us understand why these feelings are so deeply engraved in us, and why we need to quarantine our past if we want to uproot these thoughts and burn the whole tree down. Don't worry, we won't be talking about technical stuff, but you might want to make a cup of coffee before we get started.

Are you ready? Great! Let's get moving.

THE REMARKABLE WAYS OF THE HUMAN BRAIN

Mary was close to her mother. They have always been friends, and nothing made her happier than to see her mom smile. But, lately, things haven't been the same. They haven't seen each other in over a month, and their phone calls were shorter and less frequent. Mary was sure something was wrong, but she could not pinpoint the exact thing. She was confused, sad, and didn't know what to do.

Every time she asked her mom if something was wrong, the answer was always the same. "Don't worry honey, I'm fine." Then she would end their conversation as soon as it started. Today, she has tried calling her a few times, but the older woman didn't answer. Mary was panicking. She had to find out what was wrong. By the time she was asking her boss for permission to leave early, she was halfway out the door heading for her parent's house.

Let me guess. You are thinking about your mom, aren't you? That's the magic with our brains. Though one of the smallest organs, the human brain is composed of billions of nerve cells called neurons. These cells are interconnected by synapses, which transmit around 5 to 50 signals a second. These signals are how thoughts are made.

But, the process is not as simple as we've explained. According to the MIT McGovern Institute for Brain Research director, Charles Jennings, it's impossible to trace a thought from beginning to end. Think of it like trying to figure out which came first, the egg or the chicken. So, to understand where thoughts come from, it's easier to consider things that stimulate or trigger the brain to start making a thought. For instance, when reading the story about Mary and her mother, you immediately thought about your own mom.

Thoughts are stored either in your conscious or subconscious mind and only retrieved when needed. When playing a chess game, you will use your conscious mind to decide which move to make next so you can beat your opponent. But, when you can't remember driving through the last 10 blocks, it shows that your subconscious mind was in use at the time.

Psychiatrists say that the work of the conscious mind is to draw information from your senses and memory, make a decision, and translate it into action. That's why after she tried to talk to her mom for a while and couldn't, Mary decided to visit her. On the contrary, the subconscious works without your permission. Think of it like a huge memory bank or encyclopedia, if you will. When using the subconscious mind, you may be thinking without knowing it. For example, if you've been driving the same route to work for years, you don't necessarily have to think about where to stop because kids are crossing. Your subconscious will take care of it. That's why an odd coyote on the road will throw you off balance. It's not supposed to be there. Your subconscious didn't factor it in.

Interesting to note that though the conscious mind is where we think and rationalize things, it's the subconscious mind that controls our actions. You see, the brain is controlled mainly by emotions and instincts to help us meet our needs and urges. This could be anything from food, thirst, safety, and even intimacy. The subconscious and conscious mind work together to determine the best action to take, but you can't outperform your image of yourself, which is stored in the subconscious mind.

Let's go back to your past experiences as a child, since that's where you developed the thoughts that you are not enough. We have established that your thoughts are triggered or stimulated by events that elicit certain emotions. We have also noted that your subconscious mind works hand in hand with your conscious mind to decide the best course of action.

Now, if you find yourself in a situation that makes you feel inadequate, such as, for instance, you weren't able to finish a job on time, or your plan didn't work, your conscious mind triggers your subconscious mind through the emotions you feel. Let me illustrate this so that it's clear.

Let's assume you are in a meeting with your boss. You've given your presentation, and you are confident the solution will work. Then your boss says, "I'm sorry. This doesn't make any sense. It won't work." The rest of the team agrees with him. It doesn't matter if you are right or wrong, but at that moment, you feel sad because they didn't believe in your idea.

Your conscious mind immediately signals your subconscious mind through neurons and says, "Hey subconscious, we're in a binder here. This is what we are feeling, and we need to know what to do. What's your suggestion?"

Immediately, your subconscious goes to work, without you even knowing that you are thinking and comes up with the best possible answer to the question. It goes back to that time you tried to help your father by giving him sound business advice, but he didn't take it, so his business never took off. Your sub also goes to that time you advised your best friend not to date that boy, but she wouldn't listen. It then connects to that other time your science project team didn't listen to your idea, or when your mom never listened to you about going to see the doctor for her cough.

Following the same pattern, the sub gives the conscious mind the answer. "Dude, you aren't good enough. That's why people don't listen to you or take your advice even when you are right." And boom…the downward spiral begins. This process takes a split second.

There is something else you need to note about your subconscious mind. It has what's called homeostatic impulse, which keeps your body at a certain temperature, keeps you breathing regularly, and keeps your heart beating at a certain rate. Through your nervous system, it maintains your body's chemicals in billions of cells to function in harmony. It does this at least most of the time.

The same way your conscious mind practices homeostasis on your body is the same way it practices it on your mind. It keeps you thinking and acting in a way that's consistent with what you have done, said, and experienced in your past.

Because you have heard and learned so often that you aren't enough, your subconscious works to ensure that this doesn't change. It has memorized your comfort zone and is working to ensure you don't leave it. That's why the thoughts and feelings that you aren't enough keep cropping up every time you are disappointed, sad, angry, or feel coerced to do something you didn't want to do.

THE BEGINNING OF CHANGE

Learning about how the subconscious and the conscious mind work is the first step in changing. The thoughts of "I'm not good enough" are deeply engraved in you, and the only way to uproot them is by first understanding where they came from, and, secondly, knowing how to access your subconscious. Like I mentioned before, knowing what to do and taking action are two different things. You still have a journey ahead of you, but don't worry, I got you. You will make it through to the other side and enjoy the proverbial rainbows and sunshine, at least most of the time.

Look deep within you and note the things that might have pushed you to believe that you weren't good enough. I understand that looking into your past can be challenging because you don't know what you will find, but it's time for the skeletons to leave the closet. You can't hide from your own thoughts. They will haunt you until you take the bull by the horns.

As scary as it seems, you have to make a conscious decision to confront your past, transmute it, and ultimately embrace the beauty of the pain and scars it brought to you. Without doing this, you will be stuck in a never-ending cycle, struggling to get out. Now that you know where to start, let's look at what you need to do to rewire your subconscious mind.

1. Stop generating negative self-fulfilling prophecies

Have you ever made a prediction about your life, and to your surprise, it came true? Maybe you were working on a project and were excited that it will be a huge success, which turned out to be true. Or perhaps you were sure it wouldn't make it out of the basement, and sure enough, it never saw the light of day. You may not be a fortune teller, but you must have made a prediction about your life or someone else that came true. This is what's referred to as self-fulfilling prophecies. Have you ever said, "I'm not holding my breath that this is the 'one,' I doubt this relationship will work out anyway," even though you were only in the first few months of dating? Strangely enough, it never worked out. Let me shine some light on why this happens.

A self-fulfilling prophecy is a belief that comes true, mostly because we are already acting as if it is already true. The thoughts of "I'm not good enough" are an example of a self-fulfilling prophecy. Whenever you feel inadequate and like you don't deserve something, or things won't work out, more often than not, they don't go your way, and your prophecy is fulfilled.

That's how the subconscious works. It keeps you in that comfort zone because that's what you are already used to. So, if you want to change your fate and outcome, the first thing you need to do is change from negative self-fulfilling prophecies to positive self-fulfilling prophecies. It seems obvious, but you'd be surprised at how many people don't do this.

I'm not talking about holding hands and chanting, though that might have its place, but about going deep into your subconscious to rework your blueprint from negative to positive. I have to warn you, though. Since you are already used to thinking in negative thought patterns, your subconscious will do whatever it takes to keep you there. You've been doing this for years, so what makes you think you can wake up one day and just switch a button and get a home run?

Of course there has to be resistance!

Your subconscious has to do whatever it takes to keep you "safe." It has to keep you where you are used to, so you don't fail. It has never experienced positive self-prophecies, so why should it trust you? That's why merely reciting empty affirmations doesn't work. Think about this. You say one thing but mean another, which cue do you think your subconscious will listen to? Your words or your emotions?

Earlier, we said that your emotions trigger your thoughts, so your subconscious will definitely go with what you are feeling and disregard what you are saying. Does that mean saying affirmations is wrong? Absolutely not! In fact, I advocate that you use affirmations, and we will go into more in-depth details with that. For now, you need to watch every thought that crosses your mind, especially the ones that make you feel that you aren't good enough, and change them into positive, self-fulfilling prophecies.

I believe this is what people mean when they say "you get what you ask for." Expect the worst, and the worst will find you. But when you expect the best, the best will also find you. From now on, let your life be a series of reruns. Every night, you go to bed tired but wake up feeling fresh and rejuvenated. The same way you let go of your fatigued state when you sleep, let go of the pain, hurt, and scars that happened to you in the past. It's all in the past. It's gone, and frankly, there isn't much you can do about it.

So, instead of carrying the baggage with you, let it go. Today is a new day, and you can prophecy better things in your life and watch them come true, which brings me to the next point.

2. Let go of the past

I get it, the past hurts, and you are in pain. But what you do with the hurt is more important than the hurt itself or the person who inflicted it. If you endlessly dwell on something that can't be changed, you continue to hurt and blame others for what happened to you. One of my favorite sayings I like to use goes like this, "holding onto resentment is like drinking poison and waiting for the other person to die." It's ONLY hurting YOU! But, exactly how do you let go of the past?

First, make a decision that you are letting go, but you can't say abracadabra and have things disappear. It has to be a conscious decision. Accept that living in pain is your choice, as is letting go. From there, express the hurt and accept how it made you feel. You can vent to a friend, or look at yourself in the mirror and tell it to yourself. You can also speak to your religious leader or a therapist. If you had a part to play in the hurt, even a little bit, acknowledge it and accept it.

Now, being a victim feels good. It feels like you are on a winning team against the world, but it also feels like the world owes you a good life and nothing is your fault. Instead, take responsibility for your happiness and stop giving the world power. Stop giving those who hurt you the power to decide if you are happy or not. I had to apply this myself, as I walked further away from my divorce. At first, I wanted people to be on "my side" and understand that I was the victim and feel sorry for me. However, I noticed that people would judge and make up their minds regardless of what I said. So, one day I decided that I was moving forward, and it didn't matter HOW I got here, and the only person that needed to know and understand was ME.

Start focusing on the here and now. If you can learn something from the movies, it's that the protagonist, though he/she faces many challenges, always emerges as a winner. You are the protagonist in your life. Like in a movie, look for a way to overcome the challenges you face so you emerge victorious. You can't undo the past, but you can gently bring yourself to the present moment. Tell yourself, "It's alright. That's in the past, and my focus is ensuring I'm happy by doing" whatever you need to do.

3. Forgive yourself

Finally, forgive yourself. I want you to reread that line. FORGIVE YOURSELF!

We rush past that, thinking, "Sure, I forgave myself." Still, when we are alone at night trying desperately to fall asleep, we replay our grand mistakes and failures in our heads, silently beating ourselves up by solidifying our negative self-fulfilling prophecies.

This has to STOP!

Realize the negative impact you are having on your life by doing this. I had so many thoughts that would plague my mind as I healed from the divorce, that I got to a place where I would literally yell, "STOP!" I had to do whatever it takes to catch myself right before I dash down the negative rabbit hole in my mind. I would then follow it by saying out loud, "I am free from that. I already lived through that hurt, and I am not repeating it. I am free, and today is a **new** day!"

You are a good person, and the people who hurt you *might* also be good. But to move on with your life, you can't continue holding on to the past. By doing this, you will start building something different and better. You will stop looking at your past pain as the only thing that defines you, and instead, start creating a future for yourself.

The world doesn't owe you anything, and the best thing you can give yourself is to accept that and start making life-changing decisions. Don't wait for manna to fall from heaven. Create it by letting go of the past and reworking your subconscious mind.

CHAPTER SUMMARY

In this chapter, we have indulged more on why you may think you aren't good enough. We covered:

- The role different parenting styles play in making you believe you aren't good enough.
- How thoughts are made and why the conscious and subconscious mind are important in helping you uncover the truth behind the thought "I'm not good enough."
- How rewiring your subconscious mind can help you overcome these feelings and thoughts.
- How to stop the cycle of negative self-fulfilling prophecies and why it's important to do so.
- Letting go of the past and what you must do if you want to move forward.
- Forgiving yourself and setting yourself free from past hurt and pain.

In the next chapter, the rubber finally meets the road. This will be a detailed explanation of the actions you need to take to overcome your feelings of "not good enough." After the next chapter, you should have enough tools and resources to expedite your journey to recovery.

CHAPTER THREE: FLATTENING THE CURVE OF DOUBT AND REMOVING THE IDENTITY MASK

EVER SINCE SHE COULD REMEMBER, LIV HAD ALWAYS BEEN on the heavier side of the scale. Her parents tried to tell her to eat a little less, but she would get angry. When they finally gave up asking her to be more active, eat less, or at least take care of herself, she felt better. But, the damage had already been done.

At school, she wasn't part of the popular group and only hung out with one person, a boy on the football team. She couldn't understand why he wanted to hang out with her, and neither could anyone else. By looking at her, she was fat, disgusting, and a glutton—everything you didn't want to be seen around with.

She tried different fad diets, but none ever worked, until she was in her last year in high school. The summer before school, she got to work. She joined a gym, reduced her calorie intake, and did whatever it took to lose the weight. By the time she was going back to school, her schoolmates couldn't recognize her. At the back of her mind, she thought she was different, felt different, and thought things would be different.

But, even after all her hard work, nobody wanted to hang out with her apart from the "delinquents." At the back of her mind, Liv told herself she didn't fit in because she wasn't enough. She wasn't enough when she was fat, and she wasn't enough now, even after losing the weight.

Fast forward to a few years later. Liv was working in an organization as a top manager. Her life seemed to be going in the right direction except for one thing: she didn't have a family. She was past thirty, unmarried, and had no kids with snotty noses that she needed to take care of. All her friends were married, and she was a bride's maid at more weddings than she cared to remember.

Her parents couldn't stop pestering her about it, but every man she met didn't seem to fit the bill, or the relationship didn't last. Maybe this wasn't meant to be. Perhaps marriage was just one of those things that she wasn't meant to enjoy. Sigh!

YOUR STORY MAY BE different from Liv's, but you may have gone through feeling not good enough for as long as she has. This means the thoughts, feelings, and anxiety associated with this has been ingrained in you for long. You want to change, but, somehow, you are still shackled in your thoughts and anxieties even when you desperately want to move on.

Like Liv, you feel stuck with the identity you have created, and because your subconscious wants to keep you comfortable, you are stuck trying to get out. You probably even made it a few steps ahead, but things didn't work out as you thought, and you went down the drain again.

So, why is it so hard to change? Why can't you seem to break the cycle and set yourself free?

Frankly, there could be a couple of reasons why, some of them external, but as you might have guessed, most are internal. For instance, people have a way of getting in their own way when they mean to move aside and make progress.

How do you get in your own way? Simple. Through the thoughts you entertain. You may be too critical and harsh towards yourself, such that when you think of getting things done, you simply give up or doubt you can handle the task. When faced with a hard task, you may talk yourself out of it, telling yourself you can't do it. You are, after all, not enough. How can you handle such a task and make it work? Impossible!

If these are old patterns, and you know you need to let them go, why do you get in the way of change? It's because change is uncomfortable! Change forces you to look at your weakness, fear, anxiety, and thoughts in their faces. For most people, that's scary.

Using the words of Mandy Hale, "change is scary, but you know what's scarier? Allowing fear to stop you from growing, evolving, and progressing." Yet, this is precisely what you and most people do.

Because of your old patterns, you create high expectations of yourself, whether it's your goals, ideas, or fantasies, and then you become so scared of not meeting them that you don't start the journey. You may want to feel good about yourself, but then fear that like Liv, you won't be accepted anyway.

This doubt and uncertainty about yourself make you procrastinate. But, because you know you aren't supposed to procrastinate, and since you genuinely want to be free, you feel uncomfortable about it, and you become reactive. That's when you suddenly swing into action, read a book or two, start writing your affirmations, and probably even join a yoga class. Soon, the energy wears off, you procrastinate some more, and give up altogether. You then start to rationalize why you should quit, why change is too hard and you can't do it, and why it's better to leave. You may even come up with what you think is a logical reason because, from where you are standing, it makes sense.

There is more certainty in where you are, it's comfortable, and you know what the outcome will be. That is, the world will prove again and again that you aren't good enough. You are used to it, so it won't be a surprise. This uncomfortable state that comes with change makes you and millions of others get in the way of change, even when you know you can't keep living like this.

You may also be motivated by negative emotions. Ideally, you may think that strong emotions such as fear, guilt, and regret would shake you off your feet and catalyze the need for lasting change. But, usually, the opposite is true. In fact, when you have been battling feelings of not good enough, negative emotions trigger you to think of everything you are doing wrong, why you can't do any better, and why you don't even deserve anything remotely close to better. I mean, if you aren't enough, why would good things happen to you?

These emotions are a horrible barrier to lasting change. Think of someone who is trying to stick to a diet, for instance. If they eat a French fry because they had a craving, they may end up feeling so bad and guilty, blame themselves and say that they are weak. For the next few days, they end up binge-eating McDonald's food not because they want to, but to drown the guilt and feel a little better. They may even comfort themselves by saying things like "it's never that serious" and "you only live once. Do what makes you happy."

Negative emotions also trigger the all-or-nothing thinking, mainly because you are overwhelmed. You may say something like, "I'll do whatever it takes to change. But, if I fail, it means I can't do it." This traps you into a no-win situation, and you end up thinking that change is unattainable because you don't stand a chance. That's why you may sign up for the gym in January and cancel your membership in March.

Another major problem is trying to deal with everything at once. Imagine you want to climb Mt. Everest. For months, you will train, hit the gym, change your eating habits, and practice carrying heavy things in your backpack to strengthen your back. When you are ready, you will start your journey following a guide.

Now, would you attempt to climb to the top in a day? Absolutely not! You'd need to rest, catch your breath, or wait for a snowstorm to pass before you continue. So, why is getting over the negative thoughts of "I'm not good enough different"? Why do you feel the need and pressure to take on the whole challenge and win, even before you train?

Not accepting that you need to take baby steps and work your way up is the problem. Start somewhere and give yourself small, specific, measurable, and attainable goals. Then work your way through until the small goal feels like second nature. From there, add another small achievable goal and work until you achieve it. Over time, these small steps become cumulative change, which is what we are after.

That's not the only problem. Let's go back to our earlier example. You want to climb Mt. Everest, but as you go higher, you realize you don't have certain tools you need to make the hike a success. Do you think you will successfully finish your mission? Probably not.

So, why is change different?

Why would you imagine you can do it without the right support to sustain the change? Changing your thought patterns requires that you equip yourself and have enough knowledge to continue the journey and transformation. The tools you use will be different from person to person, but the bottom line is that you can't do much without the right tools. These include anything from getting a mentor, doing the required mental work, knowing what to do, and building the zeal you need to sustain the journey. That's where books like this one come in handy and if you are a spiritual person, going to church and speaking with a pastor may be of help too.

Like most people, you may also create imaginary shoes you need to fill. So, the cycle of trying and failing keeps reaffirming the thoughts that you aren't good enough. Whenever you want to change, you hesitate because you aren't sure if it will go the same way it did last time you tried to change. These imaginary shoes are sometimes created by the image that friends and family have about you. They think you should be a certain way, based on their opinion on who they think you are. Either way, you end up not filling these shoes, because deep down, you know they are robbing you of who you truly are.

To heal the past, you need to stop trying to be someone you aren't by getting rid of the imaginary shoes and taking off the mask that's been hiding your true identity. Question yourself on who YOU really are, and who you want to become in the future. Identify what you want to accomplish, and make a plan of how to do it. As we mentioned in the last two chapters, the journey starts when you heal the past.

HOW TO HEAL THE PAST

In the last two chapters, we looked briefly at how to start the journey into healing your past. In this section, however, we will dive deep into these murky waters. It's said that "until you heal your past, your life patterns and relationships will continue to be the same. It's just the faces that change."

1. Get closure

The reason you are sensitive to your past events is likely because you don't have closure. I'm not talking about spending time and money on a therapist for a few years as you try to uncover every childhood trauma and pain that may have led to where you are. Not at all. In fact, such endless plowing into your past will keep you looking behind and wishing things were better rather than move forward.

What you need to do is get active and start putting past events behind you. It could start with something as simple as saying, "I'm done. It's time to move forwards" or what people occasionally refer to as being fed up with holding the past too tightly and firmly to your heart like a well-guarded secret. If you were bullied, for instance, or had a parent who was an addict or narcissist, you may not have had an opportunity to say what you want and find peace with the situation.

For example, Liv may not have said what she really thought to her parents when they body-shamed her. Instead of giving her the tools and encouragement she needed, they, in kind or harsh words or looks, told her what everyone thought about her. This only affirmed her fear and emotional belief that, as long as she was fat, she wasn't enough.

Another way to get closure is to look at the past through the glasses you are wearing right now. You remember what we said in chapter one, kids can't understand what an adult means when they say and do certain things. Now that you are all grown up, look back at events that caused you the most pain and put yourself in the shoes of the person instigating the pain.

If your parents were too busy looking after your sibling

with special needs, leaving you to fend for yourself, you would now understand that they meant well for you, but your sibling needed more attention, work, and money than you did. Remember the numerous trips to the hospital, the time your sibling fell off a flight of stairs or the time a garbage truck scared them into crying for hours, while your mom desperately tried to calm them down.

Honestly speaking, if you were in your mother's shoes, you'd probably do the same. You'd invest a lot of your time and effort in the special needs kid because they need you more than the other child does.

How about your father, who dismissed your business idea? Maybe the approach was too simplistic and didn't fit the company model. For instance, if his company sold products wholesale, it may take up to 90 days for suppliers to pay him. Still, you were busy advising him to sell his goods on a cash basis instead of surviving on loans, overdrafts, and invoice factoring, terms you probably only learned when you went to business school.

I knew I had finally healed from my divorce when my mom and I were talking one day, and she said, "He never really loved you!" and for the first time, those words didn't cut me to the bone. Instead, I replied almost without thinking, "He did love me, the best he could. It's just that his love came from a very broken place." Moments after saying it, I smiled, because I recognized that I was healing in a way that was causing me to grow, change, and appreciate my life.

2. Get the necessary tools to manage your reactions

When anxiety begins to overwhelm you, and you are about to run down the rabbit hole, you need tools to help you manage your reactions. The first tool is looking for ways to let go of victim mentality thinking what, "they should have done… if only it had been different… or they have damaged you, and it's their fault!"

Every time you think in those terms, you end up feeling worse than you did before. It doesn't offer you anything, but only sends signals to your subconscious mind to feed the conviction that you aren't good enough, keeping you chained in place. Your subconscious thinks it's keeping you safe by helping you feed on the negative emotions and remain comfortable in what you "know and love," but that's not the case. Things are only getting worse.

So, look for ways to keep yourself calm when anxieties are fighting to take over. Look for ways to feel empowered, and act like the world is your playground, ready to soak up every positive vibe you have. This could be anything from dancing, yoga, and deep breathing. Secondly, get active and change your body position.

Wait…what?

Yes! Change your body position.

Think about this. When you are sad, discouraged, and feeling down, you often walk around with your head and shoulders down, eyes squinting. When you are happy, your shoulders are up, there's a smile on your face, and spring to your steps. So, do this deliberately when you feel sad. Stand up, do a few shoulder rolls, force a smile on your face, and widen your eyes. It will feel uncomfortable at first, but the more you do it, the more natural it becomes, and the easier it is to get your mood back up. Most importantly, it will stop the negative downward spiral.

So again, put on your "grownup glasses" and look at the situation from a different angle. First, not all of your business ideas will bypass the boss. What may be a good idea to you, may sound like a horrible idea to someone else. Second, you probably overlooked something, or your plan may be too expensive for the company right now. Maybe your colleague already has a better idea that's easier to implement without running the company into the ground.

Whatever the reason is, don't take it personally. Instead, go back to the drawing board and look for a new idea. The world is full of ideas and if you seek, you will find. If you knock, the door will be opened for you. Don't tire, keep seeking, and knocking.

I'm also a big believer in "what you sow you reap," which is God's principle not mine, but it works. I have found that sometimes the quickest way to snap out of my depressive funk or anxious mood is to "give back." I will deliberately find someone to help. For instance, carry an older lady's groceries, encourage the barista with a few kind words, or call someone I know is going through a tough time and let them talk about their problem. I will pray with them if needed. I don't mention what I am going through.

By giving back, the strangest thing will happen. I start experiencing joy, and my attention is no longer on me, what I lack, or feel. Instead, my heart starts to have a sense of fulfillment. Don't take my word for it, just try it next time you are struggling and see.

3. Change your coping mechanisms

Your reaction and triggers of the past are driven by your unconscious coping style, developed when you were a little child. It may have worked then, but it's time to rethink this style of coping because it only keeps these childhood feelings alive and makes you view the world from a child's perspective.

As mentioned earlier, start viewing the world from an adult's point of view and start taking adult actions when things happen. For instance, Liv will understand that her parents want grandkids, which may be why they are pressuring her to get married as soon as possible. Maybe they are advanced in age and fear that they will die before celebrating with her the joy of being married and having kids.

The whole situation is probably not about her, but about them. This way, she doesn't need to go on autopilot every time she sees a couple hold hands, or her friends playing with their kids. Instead, she can smile and be happy for them because soon, it will be her turn to share love with a partner. Next time your supervisor asks why your report is late, don't get defensive and irritable. Respond as an adult, calmly, and apologize for being late, then explain why you haven't turned it in. Better yet, send your supervisor a message with why the report is late even before they ask you about it.

You should also shed old identities where you stop seeing yourself as wounded, broken, needy or hurt. Shed your thinking that you're incompetent, need to change yourself, or improve something so you can be enough. All these identities limit you from seeing your brilliance. Looking at yourself through this mirror is like walking around with a blindfold on. By removing the blindfold, you see clearly. This blindfold is mostly driven by self-doubt.

Since this chapter already introduced what this feels like and where it comes from, and why it's limiting, let's go straight to overcoming self-doubt.

HOW TO OVERCOME SELF-DOUBT

Most people doubt themselves because, when looking for answers, they tend to look outside instead of inside. They use others as a guide and give them the power to dictate how they live. Everyone else is "enough," prettier, more complete, deserving, and so on. So, how do you overcome self-doubt?

1. Understand it is part of human nature

Falling flat on your face is not fun, that's why everyone has self-doubt to some degree. It protects you from falling and hurting yourself, so stop beating yourself when you doubt yourself. Instead, befriend your inner feelings and accept they are part of life, acknowledging that self-doubt is just trying to help you out. Accept that it has power over you because you are human and you make mistakes. So, doubting yourself is normal and there's nothing wrong with it, what you do next is what really matters.

A little trick I learned here is to doubt my doubts too. Since self-doubts are just my fears manifesting, they made me lose out on what I could gain because I was afraid. So, when I was in doubt, I'd doubt the doubts. My doubts are not the truth, and I learned not to treat them as if they were. I would tell myself things like, "what if the opposite is the truth? What if I'm ready?" and so on. Next time your boss gives you a bigger role to play in the team, smile and accept the challenge, and then deal with the doubt later. Fight it by first doubting the doubt, then stop making excuses.

When you are in doubt, you rationalize your situation to fit your emotional state. You are afraid you'll look bad or take on more than you can handle. Naturally, you start making an excuse as to why you can't do it. Your enemy becomes your chattering brain, and if you give it an opportunity, the default setting is to start producing excuses why you should let yet another opportunity go.

Next time you are presented with an opportunity, and your brain immediately fires up to say you can't do it, think of all the other opportunities you trashed because you thought you couldn't handle them, but you could. What reasons did you give yourself? Most weren't legitimate and were only barriers that held you back. Also, think of it this way, "If my boss thinks I can handle more responsibility, he must be right. How else did he become a boss, otherwise?".

This kind of thinking will give you the oomph and push you need to give the opportunity a try.

2. Call out your inner critic

Everyone has a negative Nancy in them, you know, that voice that's quick to remind you of all your failures, mistakes, and reasons why you aren't good enough. Like doubt, negative Nancy is part of life, and you can't silence it for good. What you can do, though, is dilute its power. You don't have to call this power "negative Nancy." You can name it whatever you want. To silence it, start by addressing it and giving it a name. For instance, you may call it Tom, Jane, or whatever else you like. Then, speak to it, preferably loudly, so you can hear yourself and your voice's power. Write it letters and tell it it's no longer running the show because it's your show and you have taken control back.

Once you have this in check, watch your inner circle. It's said that birds of a feather flock together and that you are an average of the five people you spend the most time with. People you spend time with will have a profound effect on you. If you look closely, they probably also have their own negative Nancys on high gear, or perhaps they try their best to make you feel better about yourself. Check which one of these two they do. If you feel worse after hanging out with them, it's time to change your circle, and if you feel better, it's time to listen to their advice. With people who bring out the best in you, you can do and achieve more as they fuel your confidence.

3. Raise your self-awareness

Take a few steps back and ask yourself what triggers your feelings of not enough. It may be a lack of skills in a certain area, the fact that you don't have a job, or the people you hang out with. Now, whenever these feelings pop up, ask yourself, "Why are these feelings coming up?". Note the answer and start doubting your doubt. If you are afraid you can't do something, is it because you don't know how it's done or because you don't think you can do it? If you lack the skills, then you know you can go out there and learn them. If you don't believe you can do it, then you know that's a lie, because the person who entrusted you with the responsibility had enough faith in you. So, believe in yourself, learn the skill, and get to work.

What happens when you fail at something? I suggest you learn to show self-compassion. Sometimes you will give a project your best, but you will fail anyway. That's ok because failure is also part of life. Instead of brooding in defeat, dissect it and see what might have caused the downfall. Napoleon Hill said "Every adversity, every failure, every heartbreak, carries with it the seed of an equal or greater benefit." Your job is to find the seed, plant it, water it, and let it germinate to fruition.

I have to warn you, though. It's easy to rely on others for input and advice, which is another way of giving up your power. Just because your boss trusts you to handle bigger responsibilities does not mean you run to him with every decision and try to include him in every step of the journey. Just because you have built a positive tribe of friends, doesn't mean you have to ask their opinion about everything you do in life.

Frankly, it's as exhausting as hanging out with someone who's always complaining. Also, you will end up with a product you didn't really create, and you will be giving away your power... again! Instead of looking outside of yourself for answers, look inside yourself, and trust that you will make the right decision. Not all advice is baggage, though, so learn to sift through the chaff, pick what you need, and trash the rest unapologetically. If opinions are like belly buttons, and everyone has one, you do too. So don't take everyone's belly button as the best while you have your own. Put yours there first.

ADDRESSING LIMITING BELIEFS

This is an integral part of your journey, because, as we already said, your thoughts are where those things started. So, how do you deal with limiting beliefs? How do you overcome them? I will give you a few pointers you can work with in this chapter, but the real juice will come in chapter four, where we will discuss thoughts and rewiring your subconscious mind. In the meantime, use these tips to start addressing your limiting beliefs.

First, write down the belief by playing detective and following your thoughts and emotions around. Discover what holds you back and also how strongly you hold each belief. You now need to acknowledge these are beliefs you formed about yourself in the past because of circumstances surrounding you, but this doesn't make the beliefs true. As real as they feel, you have to either defend the beliefs or achieve your goals and desires. If you argue for your limitations, you get to keep them. But you also get to lose the possibility of succeeding and finally being free to enjoy your desires and success that comes with achieving your goals.

Using your imagination, believe something different. For example, tell yourself, "I've let so many great opportunities pass, I've learned how to identify when I'm self-sabotaging" or "Now that I've been in an unhappy marriage, I know that happiness comes from within, and my partner's job is not to complete me but complement me and my happiness." Tell yourself this enough times, the same way you told yourself you aren't enough, and you will start believing it. But, saying something to yourself is not enough. Instead, go a step ahead and feel it.

Now, it's time to take action and do something different. You may be scared out of your mind, but start acting as a true embodiment of who you want to be. If you are the best at your job, how do you act when working on projects? What feelings do you have, and what do you tell yourself about the project and yourself? If you had the best marriage ever, how would you act around your partner? If you are the kind of person who lives an alternative green life, where would you shop, and what items would you pick? Not taking action on your new beliefs only re-enforces the old beliefs. So, this step is critical to your growth.

CHAPTER SUMMARY

In this chapter, you've finally started doing what it takes to get over your feelings of not being good enough. We have learned that:

- People find it hard to change because change is uncomfortable.
- The ideas you have of yourself and others have of you make it hard to change when they seem to run counter to who you are.
- It's better to start with small steps as opposed to dealing with the whole mess at once.
- Get closure, the necessary tools to manage your reactions, and change your coping mechanisms to heal your past.
- Understand that dwelling on the past is part of human nature.

- Call out your inner critic and raise your self awareness to overcome self-doubt.
- Start writing down your new beliefs, use your imagination, and take action to get over limiting beliefs.

In the next chapter, we will dive deep into understanding the brain, how to change our thoughts, and how to use affirmations to help you in this journey.

CHAPTER FOUR: REOPENING PHASE ONE—EVERYTHING STARTS WITH YOUR THOUGHTS

"THEY DON'T HIRE SINGLE FEMALES, NEVER MIND YOUNG single females," said one of the guy auctioneers to me as I questioned him about possibly applying for the prestigious job of selling art for his company. If I got it, my 6-week contracts would be spent on cruise ships sailing around the world while I hosted their art auctions and managed the gallery on board.

You might be thinking, "who buys art on a cruise ship?" LOTS of people! You have a "captive audience," so to speak. This company had such massive buying power, they were able to get it at much lower costs than most galleries, which in turn resulted in great buys onboard. But first I had to actually GET the job, which, as a 23-year-old single lady I was told was impossible! Discrimination because I was a woman? Yip. But then it was only the year 2000!

How I landed the job and managed to survive to work for a misogynist is another story altogether. For the first three years of my career, I was repeatedly told by him that I was a woman who could never "handle the larger ships." The larger ships were double the number of passengers with huge galleries and $200K budgets, which meant a 5% commission if I reached the budget. You do the math!

I worked incredibly hard at my craft to become the best, and I loved what I did every time I stepped on stage. Until I had to make the dreaded phone call to the boss after each auction, regardless of how I did, his calls were belittling, manipulative, and filled me with doubts.

But using these tools, I persevered, I began to thrive against all the odds and made incredible money, and also found myself, my strength, my courage, and my talents. I become one of only three people in the world to sell 1.8 million dollars in a single cruise and the only female auctioneer ever to go over 1 million! This is not to brag; it's to prove to you that YOU CAN TOO! Make no excuses.

We all have different ways we view the world. Some people will have a strong sense of smell and be calmed by a walk through a beautiful flower garden as they smell the roses, while others may be visual and enjoy the view up a mountain. While the mountains elicit calmness, a fight at home will trigger anxiety and stress.

Your five senses are a way to connect with the world around you. They affect how you experience events, how you interact with people, and your reaction to situations. Besides your senses, the balance between your thoughts and emotions influence how you interact with the world. Let's imagine your friend has asked you to take her to the pet orphanage. As soon as you visit the puppies, a little fellow stares at you and wags his tail happily before he is distracted by a plastic toy. He then runs in circles as he chases his tail playfully, licking and chewing on the toy. You laugh in fascination, and your heart is filled with feelings of longing. These feelings are so strong that you take the puppy home. You already have a dog, but you just couldn't resist this one. On the other hand, your friend smiled at the pup's goofiness and walked away laughing, urging you to come along to the cat section. After walking around for some minutes, she went home without a pet.

Emotions play an essential role in how you think and behave. Each emotion you feel compels you to take action and influences the decisions you make in your life, whether the decisions are large or small. To understand how these two are related, let's first understand the components of an emotion.

First, there is the subject component, which refers to how you experience an emotion. Second, we have the physical part, which is how your body reacts to the emotions, and lastly, the expressive component or how you behave in response to the emotion.

Now, some emotions can be short-lived. For example, a co-worker who is used to taking your stapler without your permission may cause you to be angry for a moment, but then the emotions dissipate as quickly as they appeared. A stapler is, after all, not such a big deal. But emotions may also be long term. You may endure long-term grief and sadness over the loss of a relationship, for instance, a breakup, divorce, or death of a spouse.

So, how are thoughts and emotions connected, and why should you care?

Your mind is a powerful tool, but like most people, you probably spend very little time thinking about it. Nobody really thinks about thinking. But, as we have already established, what you think about yourself turns into your reality. In short, what you think directly influences how you behave.

You may have heard the famous quote by Henry Ford, "whatever you think you can, or you think you can't, you are right." So, if you think you aren't enough, or that you are a failure, you will act like you aren't enough and like a failure. This enforces your belief that you are a failure and not enough.

Let's think of that time you wanted to advance your career, but you thought you weren't good enough. How did you feel? The thoughts running through your mind were probably negative and you must have felt low, sad, and anxious. You already assumed that you would fail, and so you behaved like a failure, and eventually failed. Think also of that time you had told your science group to do one thing instead of another during a project. Because you already felt like you aren't good enough, you knew they wouldn't listen to you and that the project would fail. And that's exactly what happened.

Feeling and thinking that you aren't good enough discourages you from putting in enough effort than you would if you thought you'd succeed. The lack of effort means you don't get that promotion, which also means you feel even worse. Next time, you put in even less effort, and you may even notice your boss starting to get angry with you, reinforcing your belief further. See how this plays out?

Think of that person who feels like they are socially awkward. During social events, they won't make any real effort to interact with others, and you will find them standing at the corner by themselves. When nobody talks to them, they feel worse, and it reinforces their belief in social awkwardness. What do you think they will do in the next social event? Probably show up late and stand in the corner again.

Because you've drawn this conclusion for so long, you are naturally bound to do two things. First, you will always look for evidence to reinforce this belief, or you will throw everything that disproves it down the drain, discounting it as a lucky streak. Think of that time you did well at something.

You were probably happy for a few seconds because you said, "I'm lucky it happened. Otherwise, I'm used to having bad things come my way" or "I was shocked it happened. This is new to me because bad things happen to me more often."

Our thoughts, therefore, deliberately and intentionally dictate everything that happens to us. Let's back it up with science.

In his book *Breaking the Habit of Being Yourself*, Dr. Joe Dispenza explains that we don't think in a vacuum. Instead, every thought is accompanied by a biochemical reaction in the brain, which triggers a specific chemical reaction in the body. Once your body receives this message, it immediately goes to work and initiates a response that matches with what the brain is thinking. Once this reaction is received, the body sends back the message to the brain, letting it know that everything that's happening is precisely what is expected.

Let me make it a little clear through an illustration. If you think a particular thought, such as remembering how cute it was when that dog was wagging its tail and chewing on the plastic toy, your brain sends a signal to your body to produce chemicals to match these thoughts. Immediately your body receives the signals, and it produces chemicals to remind you how you felt and then send a signal back to the brain that what you are feeling is exactly what the brain is thinking about.

All these messages and chemical reactions happen through your body's neurotransmitters, neuropeptides, and hormones.

Now, the same process happens every time you think you aren't good enough. Each time, your brain sends a signal to your body to produce more chemicals that match with what you are thinking and, like an obedient servant, your body obeys. That's why you feel sad, anxious, depressed, or other negative emotions when these thoughts cross your mind.

This creates what Dr. Dispenza referred to as the cycle of thinking and feeling. Your thoughts and feelings cannot be separated. The relationship between your body and your brain is such that when you think, the brain triggers the production of chemicals that cause your feelings to match your thoughts. Once this happens, your body sends a signal to your brain and you start to think about how you are feeling. This cycle creates a kind of loop, which is what we refer to as a "state of being."

This brings us to the conclusion that to change how you are feeling, you must first change how you think, and to change how you think, you must change how you feel. Thoughts and feelings are intertwined and can't be separated.

But, is it easy to change how you think? Is the process that easy?

The answer is a little more complicated than that, but on face value, yes, it's as simple as that. Let's dive deeper, so you know exactly what to do.

Every person thinks around 70,000 thoughts a day. That's a lot of thoughts. Most of these thoughts are a repetition of what you thought about yesterday, last year, and sometimes even ten years ago. Think about it, if you started thinking that you weren't good enough some thirty years ago, you have had this thought cross your mind several times a day for the last thirty years.

Seventy thousand thoughts a day seem even worse when your thoughts are mostly discouraging, self-defeating, unproductive, and a general waste of energy. Since you have been letting your thoughts run wild, it's time to stop the cycle and take control. After all, why should you let your thoughts control you when you can control them? It is your mind and your thoughts! You should have the final say.

From what we have learned from Dr. Joe Dispenza, you can change your life if you change your thoughts, but imagine keeping track of all 70k thoughts you have to ensure you aren't thinking negative thoughts! That's a lot of thoughts to track and, frankly, it takes enough effort to track your work, without even considering tracking all your thoughts too. Before we get to how to become a master of your mind, let's first consider and uproot the unwanted "squatters" living in your mind. We will only consider the four most notorious squatters.

1. The inner critic

We have already touched on this earlier in the book, but it is worth mentioning again. Your inner critic is your constant abuser, fueled by other people's words, especially your parents' or your caregiver growing up. Your inner critic is also fueled by the thoughts you have about yourself, the ones you have built based on what others think about you, and what you think about yourself. Comparing yourself to others, things you told yourself because of the painful experiences you've had, such as betrayals and rejection, also come in here.

As you can see, your inner critic is motivated majorly by lack of acceptance, pain, lack of self-love, and self-confidence.

2. Worry

Worry lives in the future. You mostly worry when a future outcome is uncertain and you desperately want it to turn out the way you want. Even after doing all you can ensure everything goes as expected, you can't guarantee you won't miss that flight, get sick, or lose your job.

However, that does not stop you thinking that if you worry, bad things will not surprise you. That's why you are comfortable knowing you aren't good enough. You don't know anything about the future will change so that you won't be caught off guard. You may think that if you worry, it will lower the chances of a dreaded outcome. Obviously, this never happens.

3. The reactor or troublemaker

The troublemaker is anything that sets you off. It could be feelings of something that happened to you in the past, a sound, or even a smell. When you are in your reactor state, you have no control of your emotional impulses, so you run on your past programming. That's why you become defensive when someone questions when you fail to deliver on your promise. You also defend your past events and the person you have become.

4. The sleep depriver

The sleep depriver comes with a few relatives. They could be anything from the inner planner who wants to make sure everything goes by the plan and that the plan has enough details to ensure nothing will go wrong along the way to the inner rehasher and ruminator and may even include worrying and your inner critic.

For most people, the sleep depriver is motivated by a reaction to silence, waking up to take care of the businesses you neglected during the day, and your inner critic and fears. Self-doubt, insecurities, anxiety, and low self-esteem also motivate your sleep depriver to action.

WHAT IT MEANS TO CONTROL YOUR THOUGHTS

With all these squatters in your mind, no wonder it's so difficult to manage your thoughts, and with them controlling as many as 70k thoughts, you can bet nothing good will come out of it. So, how do you control your thoughts? You observe your thoughts.

All 70k of them!

I know, those are a lot of thoughts to go through, but there is an easy way to note what you are thinking. First, check your emotions. Remember, we said your emotions couldn't be separated from your thoughts, so the easiest way to notice if you are thinking about being unworthy is to check if that's how you are feeling. If it is, you know you need to change your feelings, and thus, your thoughts.

Let's assume you have a report due for work. You are meant to work on it right now, but you are procrastinating and feel bored and unmotivated to start working. Instead, you go off to the kitchen to look for some coffee, then notice your counter is not neat, so you make a cup of coffee and start cleaning the counter. By the time you are done, a few hours have gone by, and you still haven't touched your report. By this time, you are feeling worse than you did earlier on, so you finally settle down to get to work.

Still, you don't have the motivation to get to work. Your mind may even start wandering off to other things, just to avoid working.

By noticing how you are feeling, you will become aware that you are gravitating towards negative thoughts. It's pretty difficult not to see how you feel, so before you attempt to monitor all 70,000 thoughts, start by monitoring your feelings.

FOUR STEPS TO CONTROLLING YOUR THOUGHTS

You are a thinker, which means you can observe your thoughts. If you can observe your thoughts, then you can control them. But, to change them, you have to pay attention to them and identify which of the four notorious squatters is running the show.

1. Learn to stop your thoughts

Learn to stop yourself from thinking, without caring if the thought was good, bad, or just utterly boring. Each day, practice to catch yourself in the middle of a thought and stop it. Once you stop, ask yourself how you are feeling, what you were thinking about and where the topic was likely to lead. It will take some practice and energy before you master this, especially when you are upset, angry, frustrated, or disgusted about something. Naturally, you will want to continue with the thought or fight on because that's what you are used to. This is obviously not a good strategy.

The angrier, frustrated, and upset you become, the deeper you sink into the rabbit hole. Think of that hot-tempered colleague of yours, or how dumb your kids act when they can't control their anger and frustration. Listen to the things they say. That's the person you become when you don't stop yourself on time.

This skill is especially important if the squatter running the show is a negative Nancy. Maybe you were calling yourself names, berating yourself, or disrespecting yourself. It might have even been that colleague we talked about earlier. Instead of continuing with your thought pattern, interrupt yourself. You can yell to yourself, "Stop it!" or "Enough!" and if your brain doesn't listen, say it aloud. Remind yourself that just because someone said something about you doesn't make it true. It doesn't matter who it was.

It may startle the people around you, but it will startle you as well, and you will stop that train of thinking. Stopping yourself mid-thought is not enough. Go ahead and replace the negative thought with something more empowering. Tell yourself, "I am..." followed by the empowering thought you want to associate yourself with.

For instance, you can say, "I am worthy. It doesn't matter what my teacher, parents, schoolmates, colleagues, and peers thought. I know I am enough."

2. Identify your negative thoughts

A few moments ago, we talked about observing your feelings so you can get to your thoughts because every feeling you have is directly related to a thought. If you identify the feeling, you can identify the thought. As you practice step 1, you will also start to notice that feelings are not the only way to identify what you are thinking. You can also start at the thought before you get to the feeling.

Honestly, sometimes the thoughts in our heads are so pronounced that you can't ignore them. For instance, you are talking with a colleague at work, and instantly, a thought about them, that's not so kind, comes to mind. Immediately, you may be tempted to jump into judgment mode and think that you are a bad person for thinking something so bad about someone else. So, you quickly dismiss the thoughts and move on to something different, promising yourself not to go down that route again.

I get it, I did it all the time, and I struggled with not judging my thoughts or myself for having them. What helped me was starting from the knowledge that thoughts are neither good nor bad. They are just that, thoughts. However, what I did with the thoughts is what brought the "right" or "wrong" element into the picture. Since you can't keep yourself from thinking, you can manage and control what happens once a thought crosses your mind.

In Martin Luther's words, it means, "You can't keep a bird from flying over your head; what you can do is prevent it from building a nest in your hair."

3. Write down your mental movie

Whenever you feel like you aren't enough, there is usually a mental tape running in your mind. It could be chewing your boss mercilessly in the office, telling her why your idea makes sense, and reminding her of the numerous times she didn't listen, and the whole department ended up in trouble. This may be a trigger to the root cause, or to where this whole idea that you aren't good enough started.

These tapes are not hard to identify if you do the first two steps well. In fact, they're easily identified because you most likely play this tape whenever something reminds you that you aren't good enough. For instance, if you argue with your boyfriend, you will think about it for a short while, but by default, you will go back to the "movie" in which you are yelling at your boss to listen to you.

Once you know which movie you play, you can finally get it out of your head. Now, that's where a pen and paper come into play. Every time you play the movie inside your head, it seems like something huge and powerful that you don't have control over. When you write it down, however, it suddenly shrinks. In your mind, you are unable to separate it from your emotions, but when you write it down, you can look at it from a distance, with no feelings attached.

Every good actor knows that using emotional recall is essential if they are to play their characters well. If you are playing a depressed character, you have to go back to your emotional bank and look for an instance where you were stressed, then recall or put yourself in the shoes again. If you do this successfully, shedding a few tears for the camera becomes easy.

This is the same thing you do every time you play a mental movie in your head. You associate yourself or put yourself in that event. Using emotional recall, you even experience the same emotions you did when the event was taking place. That's why the brain doesn't know if something is happening in the future or right now! If you can feel it, it is happening!

When you write it down, you remove yourself from the event, which gives you time to look at the situation from the outside. You are not as vested as you would playing the mental movie, which acts to calm you down.

4. Identify the lie and replace it with the truth

The only way to combat a lie is to replace it with the truth. Behind every negative mental state is a lie you have believed all your life, whether consciously or unconsciously. Usually, you tell yourself lies in five major areas in your life;

- Money
- Yourself or who you are as a person
- Relationships
- Your health and fitness
- Spirituality

Write down all the lies on a piece of paper and skip a few lines after each lie. Lies could be anything you believe, such as "I'm not good enough," "money is hard to earn," "I can't get a job where I'm paid what I deserve," "my family doesn't like me," or "nobody understands me." Use a pencil during this exercise. Once you are sure you have all the lies noted down, use a pen to write down the truth just below the lie. For a week, read both the lie and the truth.

You will notice that when a lie comes up, like switching a button, the truth will also come up. This is what we want. When you interrupt your thoughts, you will counter the lie with the truth each time. Now, after a week, take an eraser and erase the lie. That's where the magic starts to happen, and why it's so important that you write the lie with a pencil.

For another week, read the truth by itself. This rewires your subconscious to drop the lie and bring up the truth whenever you need it. This exercise may take over two weeks, but don't give up, no matter how long it takes you. Remember, it didn't take you two weeks to believe the lie. It took years, so don't expect the reverse to work like clockwork. Even months after you start, you may find your subconscious bringing up a lie every once in a while, but because you know what to do, it will be easier to uproot the lie.

While doing this exercise, you will be faced with two major challenges. You'll have to face your darkest fear and face all the emotions and thoughts you don't want to come face-to-face with. Secondly, you will be tempted to procrastinate. I don't mean you need to do the whole exercise in a day. It may be emotionally draining, so you may need a break to gather your thoughts and stability. But, if you take more than a two-days break, you are procrastinating. Get off that couch and continue with the exercise.

One last thing to keep in mind. When you were a kid, every time someone said you were stupid, you probably said, "I'm not stupid." During this exercise, you will be writing your truth in a different way. You see, if you say "I'm not stupid," you are still using the negative aspect of the statement (the word stupid) to describe yourself. Instead, you should use something more empowering and positive. For instance, the truth for "I'm stupid," can be "I'm bright, a fast thinker, and analytical."

THE ROLE OF AFFIRMATIONS AND WHY YOU SHOULD USE THEM

There is a lot of information about affirmations available. Some people claim they don't work while others advocate for them. I believe they work and I'm about to show you why.

Most people who say that affirmations don't work believe that there is a conflict between what you believe and the affirmations you are saying. Your self-talk is also said to be a contributor, mostly because you may think of one thing but tell yourself something different. For instance, you may affirm, "I'm worth it," then tell yourself, "That's not true, I'm not enough."

That's why you may write your affirmations in a card and read them as often as possible, but nothing happens. There is no magic, rainbows, glitters, and fireworks. Nothing!

But, and I want to make this very clear, the problem is not with the affirmation. In fact, most people who use these methods often think they are using affirmation, but they are actually using positive thinking.

There is nothing wrong with positive thinking and it does have its place in the world. So, you must understand the subtle difference between affirmations and positive thinking before attempting to use either.

You see, both affirmations and positive thinking are systems, but when done right, affirmations help rewire your brain, so that, over time, you can do things differently and believe different things.

Positive thinking incorporates the redirection of negative thoughts into more positive ones. It's a way to keep your thoughts positive and energized towards a goal or desire you have. What makes it impossible to get results is whitewashing a mountain of negative thoughts (remember the 70k thoughts we talked about) with a few positive thoughts.

Positive thoughts usually reach the conscious mind. When you interrupt your thoughts, for instance, and replace them with a positive one, you are using positive thinking. This is the first step we talked about in the last section. It's essential, but it's not the end of the road.

Think all the positive thoughts you want, turn blue while doing it if you may, but without affirmations, you won't reach and influence your subconscious mind. Yet, this is where you need to do all the weeding and uprooting, if you are to truly change your life.

So, how do you use affirmations?

Let's go back for a moment. At the beginning of this chapter, we said every thought is connected to an emotion, and the easiest way to get to your thoughts is through emotions. If you want your affirmations to work, then you must include feelings.

Feelings are the secret ingredient!

The same way you have been riding on the wave of anger, depression, anxiety, and sadness, you have to reprogram your subconscious to start riding on the waves of joy, peace, happiness, excitement, and relief.

Feelings go down to your subconscious mind. So, the same way you sent these negative feelings to your subconscious is the same way you send positive feelings. Let me remind you of another interesting fact we said about your subconscious. Your conscious mind can refuse and sift through thoughts and ideas, but your subconscious mind doesn't. Instead, it accepts what you feel and believe as the gospel truth. This makes affirmations the easiest way to access your subconscious and by far the most powerful way to influence it to change your future.

It's said that "you don't get what you want, you get what you are." That's what this statement means. If you feel you are unworthy, you get to feel more unworthy. So, if you change our subconscious path to a positive one, then you will start getting more positives out of life.

According to Dr. Dispenza, you can't think greater than you feel, which simply means that if you feel like crap, you will think the same. Kind of like "garbage in, garbage out." If you feel like garbage, you think like garbage, and produce garbage.

Your feelings are the weak link. So, when you say "I am free," you have to imagine how it feels to be free and feel the feeling of being free. If you say "I am enough," you have to feel enough and feel it in your bones.

Affirmations will signal new feelings to your brain and begin to rewrite the program that's been running your life into a new and infinitely better pattern. Now that you know how to use affirmation, don't go out and start practicing yet. Instead, start by deciding exactly what you want. Make it specific and write it down. "I want to be enough" doesn't cut it here. Define enough and what it means to you. Use specific items you can see and quantify. Something like "I want long-term friends who share the same hobbies I have" or "I want to earn $100,000 a month" or whatever else you desire.

Next, determine how you would feel if this desire came true. Would you be happy or excited? Will you feel relieved, grateful, or elated? Whatever the feeling is, connect it to your affirmation.

Your affirmation will look something like this: "I am excited I (your desire)." For instance, "I am happy my boss understood my idea and can't wait to start working on it together!"

Finally, what would you do if your desire comes true? Would you go out, call your mother, or take a trip to the Bahamas? What would you tell your mother?

Now, put everything into a mental movie, like the one you play yourself when things go wrong. The same way you practiced playing the negative movie, practice playing the positive one. Speak your affirmation mentally, inject your feelings, and have your movie play.

Even if you do it a few minutes a day, every morning, noon, night, or when stuck in traffic, it really doesn't matter. Just do it! Remember also, your subconscious does not know if the thing you affirm is happening right now, happened a few years ago, or hasn't happened yet. That's why you have been living your past over and over again through thoughts and feelings.

So, by affirming positively, you start living your future today, in faith and anticipation. Let me caution you, though. You have to dissipate every ounce of doubt, which is where your conscious mind comes to play. Every time you use affirmations, especially when you start, your conscious mind will be tempted to stop you with logic. "That's not true. You can't make $100,000 a month." Interrupt it immediately without judging or suppressing the thought.

I usually say, "That's ok, I expected that thought to come up because that's the program my mind has known for years. But now, we are working on a different frequency, one of joy, peace, and love, and in that frequency, I have a job I love that pays me $100,000 a month. I am so happy and grateful for it."

Remember the lie and truth exercise I spoke of in the last section? The second week you'll be reading the truth only. Make sure you use the knowledge in this section so you can rewire your subconscious mind. I have also included a list of twenty powerful affirmations for you at the beginning of this book if you would like to download them to get you started.

CHAPTER SUMMARY

In this chapter, we have learned:

- Thoughts and emotions are connected, and the easiest way to know what you are thinking is to check how you are feeling.
- You go through around 70,000 thoughts a day.
- Five strategies to help you change your thoughts patterns.
- Positive thinking is different from affirmations.
- Affirmations fail to work when you don't use your feelings and visualization.

In the next chapter you will learn about commitment, passion, growth, and purpose.

CHAPTER FIVE: REOPENING PHASE TWO—COMMITMENT TO GROWTH, PASSION, AND PURPOSE

JIM WAS ABOUT TO TURN THIRTY. HE WAS SEATED IN HIS car, staring at the sunset, watching it slowly sink into the ocean. In the trunk of his vehicle were all his belongings, or at least what he could salvage. His wife and three kids were back at her mother's place, leaving him to find a way out of this mess. Jim didn't mind. In fact, it was his idea that they move in back with her.

Since he could remember, he had never held a job for more than three months, and although they had survived for years with the little he had, things had taken a bad turn. He was broke, broken, and now alone with nothing but his thoughts. For once, Jim realized just how rotten his mental state was and, as he sat there watching the sunset, he decided to start by changing his thinking. He had always thought of this as people selling propaganda, but if millions said it works, they must know something, right?

Every morning, Jim would drive to the beach for his morning run and meditation, usually when it was still dark.

By first light, he was already smartly dressed and heading out to look for work. His first gig was as a waiter, and he couldn't have been happier with it. Jim even called his wife to celebrate. Because he was so good at his job, he was quickly promoted to a manager and was finally able to afford an apartment. Still, Jim maintained his morning routine, jogging and saying his affirmations. On top of this, he started repaying his debts and saving a little.

Within a few years, Jim was finally able to open his own restaurant, a small cozy place in the neighborhood. As things got busy at work, he reduced the amount of time he spent on his morning routine and eventually stopped. Jim just didn't have the time. His days became more stressful, and he started fighting with his workers, clients, and everyone who crossed his path. As the chaos got worse, Jim's business suffered, and he eventually found himself in the same spot where he had begun his journey.

Slowly, Jim started picking himself up. He sold his house and moved into a motel. He sold his business and settled some debt, then used what he had left as a down payment for a new place where he set up a smaller restaurant.

I know this seems like another cheesy story, but think of how many times you have done this yourself. You started on a high note, but somewhere along the way, you dropped everything and thought you had it covered, only for life to prove to you that you didn't "get it." Think of that time you started saying your affirmations, things started looking up, and suddenly, you felt like you owned the world. You forgot about your affirmations, and now, you ended up back to where you started. Let me illustrate.

I'm sure you've been to a wedding ceremony, and the most exciting part for most people, besides dancing, was when the couple getting married were saying their vows. "I take you to be my (wife/husband), to have and to hold from this day forward, for better or worse, for richer, for poorer, in sickness and in health, to love and to cherish, from this day forward until death do us part." Beautiful words, beautiful ceremony, and nobody goes into this waiting to get a divorce. Everyone wants to have a long, happy marriage. But, in some cases, like in mine, things don't work out.

It's the same with our personal growth journey. When you start this journey, you are excited and happy, finally glad you are doing something just for you, something that makes you happy and builds yourself to become the best version of yourself. But, along the way, especially when things get tough, you will be tempted to go back to your former default settings and give up because life is giving you more lemons, and you've had enough lemonade to last you a lifetime.

Making a solid commitment to continue with this journey till death does you part from it isn't easy. You have to wake up every day and repeat your affirmations, even when you don't feel like you are up to it. You have to fight off every thought that's trying to creep back in and remind yourself that this isn't a week or one-month thing. It's a lifetime commitment.

Life can get in the way. You will have unexpected events crop up that will destabilize you. For instance, even after doing all you can to deliver at your job, your boss may still fire you at the first instance they get. Or you may become so good at your job that the added responsibilities keep you off track, focusing on what needs to get done at work instead of your own life.

The biggest problem I've noticed with most people during the personal development journey is that they don't take action. Sometimes, their efforts aren't consistent over a long period, so they never get to experience the fruits of their labor.

To be honest, I understand why. Consistence isn't exactly

an enticing and exciting word, but like in any other area of your life, it's what will give you real results in life. Don't just be inspired to do something, get off your couch, and get down and dirty.

Tony Robbins says, "the path to success is to take massive, determined action," and that "in essence, if we want to direct our lives, we must take control of our consistent actions. It's not what we do once in a while that shapes our lives, but what we do consistently." So, saying your affirmations once in a while will not shape your life. Going for a jog once in a while won't shape your body. Praying once in a while won't shape your soul. Instead, not saying your affirmations, continuing to eat junk, and not believing in your spirituality will determine the kind of life you live.

If consistency is so important, why don't people commit? Why is it so hard for most people?

Human beings are proud. You want to continuously strive for meaning and purpose in everything you do, and when this is not met, you feel that everything you did was in vain. You have a natural tendency to be proud, entitled, and selfish. This isn't always a bad thing, but too much of it leaves you falling back into the very thing you are trying to get away from.

Secondly, you may be afraid of risk, so you put a hold on what you are supposed to do, so you don't mess up. You try as much as possible to take a step at a time to ensure you have everything under control. But you forget that, much like scientists, you may have to fail a few times before you finally get things right. Think of that baby who's learning how to walk. They stumble a few times and land on their butt. But, instead of giving up, they stand up again and try before they finally get the hang of it.

Thirdly, because you understand that there is risk involved, you want to have a fall-back plan. You want to know that there is a safety net somewhere waiting to catch you. This gives you comfort, but you don't realize that it's dividing your energy, so you don't entirely focus on the journey. In some cases, you may even give the fall back plan more attention than you do the main plan, which is setting yourself up to fail.

There is also the issue of comparing yourself with others. Comparison will do one of two things. It will make you feel less than another person, which is what happens to most people, or make you feel better than others. When you've been battling with feelings of not feeling good enough, you are likely to sink down the rabbit hole when you compare yourself with others. Feelings of low self-worth and low self-esteem emerge, and you even start thinking about giving up on your journey. You are, after all, not good enough.

Feeling better than others doesn't do you any good either. In fact, it's as damaging as feeling less than someone else. You see, you are tempted to place judgment on others, so your accomplishment and worth is directly related to certain ranks you've set in your life.

The quote, "aim for the moon. If you miss, you'll land among the stars" is meant to caution you against having unrealistic expectations. But, on the other hand, you are encouraged to aim high. So, let your goals scare you, then do whatever it takes to attain them. When you have unrealistic expectations, you are dishonest with yourself, and you may be putting yourself up to fail. If you fail, you will, as if by default, go back to thinking that you failed because you aren't good enough.

So, how do you stay committed to your growth?

HOW TO STAY COMMITTED TO GROWTH

1. Use the 20-20-20 formula

This formula was first invented by Robin Sharma, who called it the formula of superhuman productivity. According to Sharma, how you start your day determines how productive you will be. He advocates that you spend the first 20 minutes of your day working out, and you can guess why. Exercise has immense value to us, including brain chemical reaction that releases feel-good hormones. It also keeps us healthy and young.

For the next twenty minutes, focus on reacting to yourself, your goals, and what you want to achieve. This is where you focus on your affirmations and writing down your goals and desires. Finally, dedicate another 20 minutes to concentrate on personal growth, such as reading a good book, listening to an inspiring podcast, or anything that inspires you to be a better person.

All this is done within the first hour of waking up. Since you have work and tons of other things you need to do, it's best to start this hour of power as early as possible. Set your alarm for 5:30 AM. Don't hit the snooze button, you'll be procrastinating again, and eventually blame your lack of commitment on not feeling good enough. Stick to getting up each day and follow this model, and you'll see the changes.

2. Work closely with a mentor

Everyone needs a little nudge every once in a while. It's even better if this nudge is coming from someone you respect and can learn from. By a mentor, I don't necessarily mean someone powerful and rich. It could simply be someone who made it through this journey or one of your most positive friends who can keep you accountable. It's a great way to keep you committed to your goals.

For this to work, come up with a suitable schedule for you and your mentor or accountability friend. For instance, you can send your friend the list of affirmations you wrote this week or today, depending on how you want to go about it. With a mentor around, you know that your desires and goals aren't for you alone and like most people, including me, you won't want to let your mentor down. Also, your mentor will believe in you and want to see you succeed. This encouragement and push will give you the nudge you need to keep moving, even when things don't seem like they are working.

Another great alternative is to be a mentor to someone. Having someone look at you as a reliable source means you have to do the work. You have to force yourself to keep moving because you know someone else is looking up to you for guidance. What I'd warn you against is doing this too early into your journey. Remember, you can't run on empty, and you can't give what you don't have.

So, first amass as much as you can before you attempt to give out to others, at least until you are a point where you can hold yourself accountable.

3. Celebrate your wins

We all want to be liked. When you post something on Facebook or Instagram, you are always looking at the notifications to see who has liked your post, and if you get any comments. That's human nature. Naturally, we form tribes and want to have people around us to celebrate with us and help us when we are in trouble.

Most of us want to be liked more than we actually like ourselves and expect others to celebrate us more than we celebrate ourselves. That's why victory at work doesn't feel like victory unless your boss tells you that you did an excellent job and, if possible, recognizes you in front of your colleagues, especially those you don't see eye to eye with.

It is important, however, that we should wake up and like ourselves first. Wake up, look in the mirror and say to yourself, "I like you, Cindy. I think you are incredible and the best thing to ever happen to this world." When you win, look in the mirror and pat yourself on the back before anyone else joins the party. Celebrate yourself for the small achievements you make, so that when the big ones happen, it won't feel awkward to you.

Also, celebrating the small wins shows you the progress you are making. You know you are moving ahead and you can do this. It's no longer out of reach, but something you can do, because you have evidence right in front of you.

When growing up, my grandfather would say, "If you don't blow your trumpet, who will?". You see, the world is always looking for an example of how to treat you. If you treat yourself kindly, the world follows. If you treat yourself with love, the world follows. If you treat yourself with poise and class, the world follows. If you celebrate yourself, the world follows. Don't wait for the world to give you what you don't have. Show the world how you want to be treated, and it will follow.

Perhaps the most important thing you need to keep in check is knowing your purpose. Now, there has been a lot of controversy around the subject, but because I know how important it is in your journey to grow, I'll demystify it and give you the truth that worked for me and hundreds of others. That's why I'm going to talk about purpose in the next section of this book.

THE NEED FOR PASSION IN LIFE

I'm sure you have once started something and left it halfway done because it just didn't tick off the right boxes for you. It doesn't matter what it was, but leaving things undone is a clear sign of a lack of passion. Steve Jobs once said, "you have to be burning with an idea, or a problem, or a wrong you want to right. If you're not passionate enough from the start, you'll never stick it out," and he was right.

His love for Apple made him wake up every day and work, doing everything he needed to do to succeed. So, why should your personal growth journey be any different? Being passionate will drive you to wake up at 5:30 AM for your 20-20-20 routine when all you really want to do is sleep. It's what will push you to stop yourself from thinking negative thoughts and to go back to the drawing board whenever you fail. Passion is the fuel you need to push you into action. Without it, the journey is another boring trip that doesn't inspire you.

When you are passionate, you are confident, and you create value for yourself and others. You will always look for a way out, and you will find it easy to lead others if you decide to be a mentor to someone else. Also, being passionate makes you excited to share your journey with others. You are happy to share your success, challenges, and everything in between. But, passion in itself is not enough to fuel the journey. You must first understand why you must get over feeling not good enough.

Why is this a matter of life and death? What do you have to lose if you don't change?

FINDING YOUR "WHY"

Let's think about Jim for a moment. Before he started his personal development journey, he had moved from job to job for years, not sure what he wanted to do with his life. He wasn't sure what his passion was, and he was probably not even sure how to start. This hopping from one job to another was also visible in other areas of his life.

Like you, he probably felt that he wasn't good enough for those jobs, or that he just couldn't put a finger on what he wanted to do with his life. Finding his passion for food was probably a little more complicated than a desperate move to look for an income.

Maybe when he was young, he would find himself in the kitchen whenever his mother was cooking. But because he was from a community that believed that "women belong in the kitchen," it was out of the question for him to pursue anything remotely close to becoming a chef. When it was finally time for him to get his life in order, he started where he knew he would thrive, excel, and deliver his best; in the kitchen.

It doesn't matter that he was starting as a waiter. As long as he had access to the kitchen where some of the best chefs were making gourmet meals, he was fine. Becoming a manager was a step towards fulfilling his dream of owning a restaurant. The position excited him because he got firsthand experience leading and working with others while under-standing the finances and business implications that come with running a successful restaurant. That certificate he studied and thought he'd never get to use was now his ticket to earning more.

Because he had found his purpose and fueled it with the burning desire to change, it was easy for him to start over when he lost everything. Besides, he only lost money, not the skills he needed to make it. That's why we have to keep learning because when you learn something, it's yours to keep.

Whether you are at a point where you are recognizing your desire for something more or you simply want to be free of all the baggage you've carried through your life, finding your purpose is the missing link between affirmations and passion.

Your "why" or passion is what describes why you are on this journey. Are you doing it because you want to save your marriage? Become a better parent? Or simply because you want to be the best version of yourself so you can help others? You have to answer the question, "I want to be good enough, but for what?" or in simpler terms, "survival for the sake of what?".

You see, animals have one purpose in life, to survive, but that isn't enough for you and me. Our human nature is such that we are always looking for something more than survival; without the answer to the above questions, we fall into disillusion, we are distracted, and we can fall into despair.

That's why so many people fall back on drugs and alcohol abuse. It is also the reason for the high numbers of people who suffer from depression, commit suicide, and rely on antidepressants. It's a means to survive. While some people who resort to these acts have underlying mental health issues, others failed over and over again to find their purpose in life.

Granted, there is not one, single pathway to knowing your purpose. The world is full of ways you can use to gain deep insight into who you are and what you want to offer. To find your sweet spot, ask yourself the following questions.

HOW TO FIND YOUR PURPOSE

1. What makes you come alive?

I'm not referring to your dream holiday or a trip to watch your favorite football team win. I'm talking about what puts fire into your belly and makes it burn with energy. Take a pen and paper and write down the activities you did that made you forget about time. If you've heard people say that "time flies when you are having fun," this is what they mean. Forgetting time as you work is what most people call 'flow'. At the heart of these activities, you will find your passion and purpose. These activities energize you and leave you feeling fulfilled and happy.

When you aren't connected to your purpose, your work leaves you drained, angry, stressed, and exhausted. Another way to find these activities is to do what Jim did. Look for something that you did as a child just for the fun of it. Look for patterns of things that tend to repeat themselves. For instance, when you were at your lowest, what's the one thing that brought you back to life? Was it cooking, drawing, writing, or something different?

When you were most comfortable and excited, which activities did you do? People tend to lose sight of what they enjoyed most when they were kids because adolescence and adulthood come with pressure. Naturally, you will be robbed of some passions, but connecting with them again will help you find your purpose.

Finally, think of all the activities you are willing to do as an adult, even when people think they are embarrassing. It could be something you have no skills and competence in, but you somehow keep going back to it, even after making tons of mistakes. The activity is so meaningful that you do it even when other people think you should drop it and move on. Avoiding things that embarrass you is natural, but when you do that, you run the chance of avoiding things that make you feel fulfilled.

2. What is your natural strength?

When you are in your element, your natural skills meet your passion. You are more productive and you add more value to others and yourself. Funnily, it's also when you tend to make the most money! Now, take the list you created in the previous point and think of the items you find so easy to do, but others find hard.

Create a new list with these items and check for patterns. Is your list falling into creative items or more technical things? Are you good at coming up with creative solutions to problems, or do you prefer to execute projects with a precision that others find tedious? Perhaps you are a natural communicator and technocrat, or you can spot when the status quo needs a makeover.

Obviously, you can also be passionate about things you have no talent in, the same way you can have little passion for something you are talented in. From my experience and that of people I have mentored, you will mostly gravitate towards what you are naturally gifted in. Howard Thurmon says, "Don't ask yourself what the world needs; ask yourself what makes you come alive, then go do that. Because what the world needs is people who have come alive." This simply means that if you focus on what you are good at, you will naturally find your place in the world and monetize your purpose.

3. What adds the most value to others?

We are innately born with the desire to help others. You will see a toddler share their toys with a homeless child, or wipe tears off another child when they fall and hurt themselves in the playground. That's why you are compelled to adopt a pet or take a stray puppy to the shelter. You may have bought a meal for a homeless person not because you wanted fame, but because you felt the need to help. It felt good, didn't it?

Being self-aware is great, but doing something for others without expecting a reward is awesome. That's why it felt so good to feed a homeless person. When you find your purpose in life, you are grateful for the life you are living, and you often contribute to the world more than those who don't have that sense of gratitude.

However, people tend to undervalue their strengths, expertise, and skills, especially if they come naturally. You often think, "it can't be that easy." In truth, it does. Go back to your list and ask yourself which problem you enjoy solving the most and which problems you are most passionate about. Is there a pattern you have noted? By now, you probably have a few items left on your list, depending on how large your list was. Use this list to check if you are passionate about the problem they solve and if the problem excites you enough to get you out of bed in the morning because you felt it helps others achieve their goals and desires. This will further narrow down your purpose.

4. Make a decision

By now, you have sifted through all the things you feel you are good at, have experience in, and come up with a short list; hopefully, not more than five items. It's now time to decide which among these you will stand for, which one is the "do or die idea." It's said that "If you don't stand for something, you easily fall for anything." This is what we want to avoid, and what we have been working through during this chapter.

Now, pick your five points and ultimately decide which is the most valuable to you. Which among these matters the most to you? Which one do you feel you can't do without? Why is it so important to you? How can you use it to add value and serve others? This question is especially important because we all need money to live. But, although money is important where it is needed, it's useless where it's not needed. To earn the most money, however, we must serve a lot of people, and the only way to help others is by adding value to their lives.

Steve Jobs, Warren Buffet, Tony Robbins, Miles Monroe, and other millionaires are only millionaires because they serve many people. They found their purpose, served more people, and thus, earned more money.

But, let's be honest. Everything sucks a little at some point in life, even that thing you are most passionate about. Just because something is your purpose does not mean you'll not get bored with it sometimes, or that challenges will be easy. Everything involves some level of sacrifice and cost. Be comfortable with the struggles and challenges that come with your purpose. Your ability to endure during rough patches determines if you are willing to stick with your chosen purpose.

If you want to be an entrepreneur, but you can't handle failure, you will have a hard time. If you're going to be a writer, artist, or musician and you can't handle your work being rejected hundreds, sometimes thousands of times, you'll be done before you start.

Keep in mind that passion and purpose are a result of action, not its cause. You won't know how you feel about an activity until you try it. So, if someone had a gun to your head, and you had to choose one thing, what would it be? Alternatively, if money wasn't a problem and you had everything you'd ever wished for, what would fill your day such that you aren't bored to death?

Go out and try these things and, eventually, you'll stand behind one and be ready to do or die. It doesn't have to take a few hours to decide, but if it takes more than a year, you are procrastinating again. Stop yourself and make a decision. Run the good race and fight the good fight. That's when you will find fulfillment.

CHAPTER SUMMARY

The most important things you need to remember from this chapter are:

- You must stay committed to your journey if you want to see results.
- Passion and action are the fuel you need to steer your journey into the right direction.
- To find your purpose, look for what makes you come alive, your natural strength, and how you will add value to others. Then, make a decision.

In the next chapter you will learn how to embrace your new normal and live life on your own terms.

CHAPTER SIX: EMBRACING YOUR NEW NORMAL

I HAD A PRETTY NORMAL CHILDHOOD. I WOULDN'T SAY there was anything extraordinary about it, except that I was born and raised in South Africa. We moved to America during my freshman year of high school. I have always been a very strong, outgoing person who could make friends easily, but I was unprepared for a California high school and the "meanness" that followed.

I had a very strong accent, and at first, everyone loved it. They even thought it was cute. But after a while, it became the thing that kids teased me about. I was called names like "bushwacker," and made fun of when I called something by a name they didn't recognize, like calling a "trashcan" a "dust-bin." There was also the very embarrassing moment when I leaned over to the boy sitting next to me and asked him if I could borrow his rubber. The kids around him heard my request and began to scream with laughter, leaving me puzzled. I didn't understand why, because I was just asking for a rubber to rub out a mistake I had made. It didn't take me long to realize you call that "an eraser" because "a rubber" means something entirely different in the States. I was also freakishly tall for my age and skinny, which gave kids even more ammunition to hurl insults at me. I used to love school but secretly began to dread going because now it seemed I went home crying more days than not.

I was raised a Christian and knew God loved me, and I was made in His image; but there is a difference between knowing something and believing it. The daily criticism and bullying I experienced wore me down and I knew I was supposed to 'turn the other cheek', but instead, I began to lash out from the pain I felt. I learned to use sarcasm that was being used against me and spun it around to belittle the boy who was the worst bully. I made the other kids laugh at him. You would think the little victory would have made me feel better. Instead, I just felt my heart harden. Who was I becoming? I was protecting myself, I told myself... but at what expense?

You've heard that expression "sarcasm always has some truth to it." What I realize now is that what hurt me so much is that deep down, I truly believed some of what they were saying about me. I had insecurities about myself, being liked, being loved, being authentic, that I covered up with my humor and big personality.

High school was a long four years. During university, I developed coping methods to hide the insecurities. For instance, I worked out like a crazy person to have a body that would be admired and not made fun of. I fixed my hair, teeth, and everything else to avoid being the brunt of jokes because I wasn't going to go through the same pain again. Not on my watch. But I never worked on my inner self. I never stopped to ask why I felt this way, and I never under-stood boundaries or that I could tell someone NO, it's not ok for you to treat me this way. Sometimes we approach our lives, friends, or boss like we are still in high school where we felt helpless against the bully.

I carried all of this into my marriage, and because I was covering up for so much, I wasn't paying attention to everything my husband was covering up for. All I will say about my marriage in this book is that some people are a lot more broken than you, but in the end, this will destroy you too if you let it. It was only after my divorce that I learned to look within for answers and to demystify some of the beliefs I had about myself and my faith. I learned to look out for myself and to believe in the decision I made for my life. It wasn't easy because we aren't naturally taught how to be selfish. In fact, we are taught the opposite.

Growing up, we learn how to please others and do whatever will make them happy from a young age. Think of any child who wants to impress his parents.

During the covid-19 pandemic, the question "are you essential" reminded me of that day laying on the bathroom mat crying, when I asked the same question of myself. It was a pivotal moment, a defining time in which I faced my doubts, my past, and the identity I wore for others. I had to choose to grow through it and find my passion and truth. I began to believe in God and the good He had planned for me, not just "knowing" about Him. This is a road less travelled, because, as I mentioned, we aren't taught how to look out for ourselves. We are told to be selfless and to only have the other person's interests at heart. While there is nothing wrong with this, we often fail to learn how to look out for ourselves, celebrate when we do things we are proud of, and even say one little word, "no."

We are told we shouldn't be selfish, and we should always share with others. That little girl at the playground will be told to share her toy with another child, and be forced to do it when she doesn't comply. As she grows, she learns that she has to share her time, resources, and whatever else she has. She doesn't learn how to say no, look out for her own interest, and be self-focused. She feels she isn't essential, because if she were, she would have been taught how to be focused on herself, how to say no, and how to choose what works for her without feeling guilty.

If you are reading this, you probably know what it means to be selfish, but do you know how to be selfish? When you hear of the word, your first thought is perhaps negative, where terms like self-centered, self-involved, and self-serving come to mind. You were taught to avoid thinking of you alone and your interests, but to live for the good of all humanity. Giving is shown as preferential to taking, but what we don't usually know is that taking is part of the process. You can't give what you don't have, and sometimes, to give you must take first.

There is a thin line between looking out for your self-interest and being unfair to others. For instance, think of an airplane or an accident. When the flight attendant gives instructions on how to use the oxygen mask, you are told first to ensure you have your mask on before you help someone else. During an accident, you are told to ensure you are safe before attempting to rescue those who are hurt. Obviously, nobody will call you selfish for following these guidelines.

Why do you feel as if you are selfish when you refuse to have your friend crash over for months at your house? Or why is it selfish and unchristian to say "no" to donating money to someone who you are sure will misuse it or enable their over the top lifestyle or their addiction?

This is what happened to Stacy. Growing up as the first-born of four siblings, she had to give up luxuries, so the younger kids would enjoy them. She was, after all, the oldest one. When she completed her education and got her first job, she took up the role of helping her parents educate her siblings. Eventually, everyone was doing fine, but things took a turn when her younger brother, the last born, dropped out of school. He complained of not being treated fairly, said he wanted to stay in an apartment, and wanted the rest of the family to send him at least $500 a week for pocket money. As if that wasn't not enough, he wanted a new car. Although her sisters were all working, they refused to help Stacy with their brother's requests, bringing Stacy to her wits' end. Her parents expected her to help her brother, as she had all her life. They accused her of being selfish for refusing to help. Stacy became stressed by the whole scenario. She started hating her job and even thought of moving to another state to get away from everyone.

Like Stacy, what you may not accept is that sometimes, being selfish is the right thing to do. Also, just because someone defines something as selfish does not mean you have to use the same guidelines. If you want to opt-out of a party, for instance, your friend might say that you are selfish for not attending, but that doesn't mean you should accept their definition.

If you don't give enough thought to yourself and your needs, clear space and time to spend alone doing what you love, or are afraid to assess your needs and desires right now, you probably need to learn how to be selfish. This also applies if you are always looking for outside validation, always feel guilty when you don't help, and feel like you owe something to someone even when you don't.

After the five chapters we have covered so far, you already know that to feel good enough, or essential, you need to strike a balance between being selfish and helping others. If you know your value and that you are enough, you will say "no" when you feel something isn't right without feeling guilty. You will turn down a party so you can spend time with yourself at the spa, and you will definitely not finance your brother's $500 weekly expense or buy him a new car because he feels he needs one.

This new normal is not going to be a walk in the park. As with any transition and change, there will be times you feel like you aren't doing the right thing, or that you are failing. What I can assure you is that you will have enough energy in the morning to fill your day with positivity and great vibes, but first, you must learn how to set boundaries and retake your power to say "no."

HOW TO SET HEALTHY BOUNDARIES

Currently, your boundaries may be strict, loose, inbetween, and in some cases, nonexistent. Most people who feel they aren't good enough or have no strong sense of self also don't have boundaries. You've probably heard the saying, "you get what you tolerate," which simply means your life isn't a result of the circumstances you go through, but a result of what you settle for, or what you allow to remain in your life.

Let's think of all the bad things your parents did to you when you were a child or the many times others mistreated you. You have carried these memories with you for so long that your default setting has been to look at yourself as a second-class citizen. You allowed them to settle in your heart and subconscious mind, and now they control your life even without you knowing.

So, since your parents had a role to play, you have to take responsibility for allowing these thoughts and feelings to dominate when you could have chosen not to. It's your decision to make, and luckily, we've already learned how to get started. As you can see, boundaries are not about limiting other people's access to your life; they include protecting yourself from one person who can hurt you the most: yourself.

Personal boundaries are actually defined as physical, emotional, and mental limits, you establish to protect yourself from being manipulated, used, and violated by others, and as we have learned, by yourself. These boundaries help us develop a clear separation of what you think and feel from others' thoughts and feelings. You can express yourself as a unique individual and acknowledge the same about others. This way, you can enjoy healthy relationships and communicate directly and honestly.

That's why it's so important to know that you are essential. Without this, you cannot set clear boundaries, preserve your integrity, take full responsibility for your individuality, and control your life. To set healthy boundaries, you need to:

1. Check where boundaries are needed

Examine if you already have boundaries so you can spot where they are lacking. For instance, you may have healthy boundaries with your colleagues but fail to have them with your spouse/romantic lover and friends. From here, you can decide the limits you need to set with your friends and spouse. When setting the boundary, let the focus remain on you, and refrain from attaching consequences, but explain why the boundary is important to you. Although you don't need to explain your decisions all the time, it's important to say why you are setting the boundary. This is especially true when you are dealing with your kids and spouse. For instance, let your spouse know why your career is important to you and why you have decided to keep working.

The bottom line is to be clear of what you need from various relationships and then set boundaries based on those desires. If the limits are clear to you, they will be clear to others.

2. Be assertive

Being assertive means being firm but kind to others. If you are pushed to be aggressive, it feels harsh and punishing. Practice being clear when you give your decision, but also ensure the person knows it's non negotiable. Also, you shouldn't blame or threaten the recipient. You can use a statement like, "I feel (feeling) when (the recipient does/says something) because (reason.) What I need is (what you'd prefer to happen.)." For instance, "I feel violated when you read my text messages because I value my privacy. What I need is privacy to speak openly to others and share my thoughts." By far, such a response is better than "Stay off my phone."

You must also trust and believe in yourself, and accept that you are the highest authority on yourself. You know what you want, why, and what you value. Stop allowing others to make that decision for you. Instead, trust in your intuition or inner voice, and go with your gut feeling. Remember, though, you can set boundaries without announcing it. For instance, put your valuables in a safe and lock it, use a password to protect your digital journal or phone, and schedule a non-negotiable timeout.

3. Get comfortable with saying "no"

I know it's daunting, especially when you think of "no" as a complete sentence. In most cases, you are tempted to say "no," then explain, but it's not always necessary. Explaining is providing emotional support to the person you are saying no to, and frankly, you don't always need to do that.

If a coworker asks you to cover their shift, you don't need to explain why you can't do it. The same goes for when someone asks you for your number or to dance with them. Saying "no" with no tagged explanation will seem weird at first, but the more you do it, the more comfortable it gets.

Start by identifying the behaviors and actions you find unacceptable, so you can let others know when they cross the line. For instance, you might hate it when someone keeps touching you when having a conversation because you feel it's an infringement of your personal space. Let them know without mincing your words. Be calm, clear, and firm. You don't have to be rude, but you should let them know how you feel.

You may have noticed that you have some significant transitions to go through during this journey of self-discovery and growth and the only way to get through it is through sheer resolve and willpower. According to numerous studies, willpower is the keystone habit for individual success. The best way to cultivate willpower and self-discipline is through making a habit, such that they become automatic.

You don't have to think about it. It comes naturally. Like other skills, you learn and strengthen your willpower. A research was conducted by psychology candidates at Case Western to discover why willpower needed to be activated every day. The researchers took candidates and gave them a bowl of freshly made cookies, oozing with chocolate chips, and another one with radishes. As a control, they gave another group the cookies without the radishes. The first group was supposed to ignore the cookies and eat the radishes, while the second group was supposed to eat the cookies. The cookie-eating group was in heaven, but their counterparts were in what you can only refer to as radish purgatory. After tasking the radish eaters' willpower, the researchers gave both groups a puzzle to solve, promising them that it won't take long and that it was a way for them to pass the time as the sensory memory of the food fades. What the participants didn't know was that the puzzle couldn't be solved. It took willpower to keep working on it, mainly because each attempt failed. They were to ring a bell and call it quits if they felt they couldn't solve it. Interestingly, the cookie eaters spent more time on the puzzle, an average of 19 minutes, and they appeared to be more relaxed than the radish eaters. In fact, the radish eaters were often frustrated, gave up easily, and even snapped at the researcher. On average, the radish eaters only spent eight minutes on the puzzle before ringing the bell.

Through the experiment, the researchers discovered that willpower is not just a skill; it's a muscle that gets tired when it's overworked. There is less willpower left for other things, if this happens. That's why good physicians can make dumb medical mistakes, or an accountant can be conned out of all of their money in broad daylight.

Like your arm muscles, you can exercise and strengthen your willpower, as proven by Megan Oaten and Ken Cheng. In their experiment, they put people through a series of tasks (exercising, saving money, and learning) and asked them to follow the programs to the letter. As the participants' self-discipline increased, other areas of their lives were also positively affected. For instance, they spent less time watching TV, worked out more (even if they weren't in the exercise experiment), smoked fewer cigarettes, and ate healthier meals.

The same thing happens during this journey. When you

force yourself to stop negative thinking habits, you also change how you think and regulate other impulses. You learn to distract yourself from temptations, and your brain learns how to help you focus on your goal. Think of a child who goes for a piano lesson. It may have nothing to do with creating the next Mozart, but as they learn to force themselves to practice for an hour, they exercise their willpower and start building their self-discipline.

So, force yourself to wake up early and do your 20-20-20 hour of power each day, even on days you don't feel like getting out of bed. The more you work out your willpower and self-discipline, the easier the journey becomes. As we mentioned, you can use your "why" to help you focus on the reward you will get for sticking it out through the journey.

One of the tricks you can use to develop self-discipline and willpower is to plan. Think of instances where you may be tempted not to follow through and what you'd do to ensure you do what's needed. Also, look at what triggers your feelings of not good enough and plan on how to respond. Ask yourself, "If my boss is dissatisfied with me, I plan to work harder." or "If I don't feel like getting up to do my morning routine, I plan to go to bed earlier."

Willpower becomes a habit when you deliberately plan your course of action ahead of time, then follow that routine when the inflection point arrives. The more time you do it, the easier it becomes, and the more it registers in your brain, especially your subconscious. If you tell yourself that you have what it takes to succeed, you will prove yourself right. Planning ahead in one area will slowly become planning in other areas, and eventually, you'll develop habits that steer your life towards the direction you want to take.

So, don't look back at what was, or think of how things would be easier if the past didn't happen the way it did.

That's water under the bridge and it won't change no matter what you do. Concentrate on making sure that your tomorrow is better than yesterday, and impart these skills in others so they can also improve their lives. The beauty of life is not having everything handed to you on a silver platter. It's working your way through your struggles to find gold and sharing the lessons you've learned along the way with others.

CHAPTER SUMMARY

In this chapter, we have learned that:

- Setting healthy boundaries is important because it directly affects how you feel and view yourself.
- Willpower and self-discipline are muscles you can exercise. The stronger they are, the easier it is for you to change and maintain the change.
- Once you have started the journey to self-discovery and growth, it's important not to look back at what was, but to focus on the future and what it holds.

∽

Leave a 1-Click Review!

I WOULD BE INCREDIBLY thankful if you could take just 60 seconds to write a brief review on Amazon, even if it is just a few sentences.

>> Click HERE to leave a quick review

FINAL WORDS

"As a man thinketh in his heart, so he is."

— PROVERBS 23:7

I grew up hearing these words, but I never really understood their meaning until I started my journey to becoming the woman I am today. Every thought I had shaped who I was, the decisions I made, and my life. It wasn't anyone's fault but my own.

I learned that if I wanted to do or have something, I had to go out and get it. Once I accepted this, my questions switched from "who will help me out of this," to "where do I get what I need to get out of this mess." I stepped up my thinking, friends, and career, and with it came joy, happiness, and prosperity.

As cliché as it seems, watch what you think about yourself, and what you tell YOU about yourself because that's really what shapes your life. If you want to change, you have to first switch your inner and outer conversations about yourself, understand that you don't need to do anything or impress anyone to be enough. You just need to be you.

The world is your oyster, and it's waiting for you to shine your light. Stop fearing what will happen or what people will say because what other people think about you is none of your business. It's more important to care about what you feel about yourself.

Like a faithful servant, wake up each morning and serve yourself a plate of fresh love, motivation, and positive affirmations before you hit the road to help others. By first filling your cup, you will have enough to give. Don't worry about failing. That's what makes the journey worth it. Just knowing you fought the good fight and ran the good race will motivate you to get up each morning and keep moving.

Besides, nobody said it was easy, but it's sure worth it. So, do whatever is required to cultivate your willpower and keep friends who will motivate you to take the bull by the horn. But, remember, it's all up to you. If you want the world to treat you well, start by treating yourself well. If you want the world to love you, start by loving yourself. The world will always follow your example of how to treat you, so be kind, loving, and respectful toward yourself. The world will follow.

"As a man thinketh in his heart, so he is." Watch what you think in your heart because that is who you will become.

Made in the USA
Monee, IL
17 December 2020